When Friends Come from Afar

WHEN FRIENDS COME FROM AFAR

*The Remarkable Story of Bernie Wong and
Chicago's Chinese American Service League*

SUSAN BLUMBERG-KASON

3 FIELDS BOOKS
An imprint of the University of Illinois Press

3 Fields Books is an imprint of the University of Illinois Press.

© 2024 by the Board of Trustees of the University of Illinois

All rights reserved

Manufactured in the United States of America

1 2 3 4 5 C P 5 4 3 2 1

♾ This book is printed on acid-free paper.

Library of Congress Cataloging-in-Publication Data

Names: Blumberg-Kason, Susan, author.

Title: When friends come from afar : the remarkable story of Bernie Wong and Chicago's Chinese American Service League / Susan Blumberg-Kason. Other titles: Remarkable story of Bernie Wong and Chicago's Chinese American Service League

Description: [Urbana, Illinois] : 3 Fields Books, an imprint of University of Illinois Press, [2024] | Includes bibliographical references and index.

Identifiers: LCCN 2024006057 (print) | LCCN 2024006058 (ebook) | ISBN 9780252046070 (cloth) | ISBN 9780252088186 (paperback) | ISBN 9780252047305 (ebook)

Subjects: LCSH: Wong, Bernie, 1943–2021 | Chinese American Service League—History. | Chinese Americans—Illinois—Chicago—Biography. | Social workers—Illinois—Chicago—Biography. | China—Emigration and immigration. | United States—Emigration and immigration. | Chinese Americans—Illinois—Chicago—Social conditions. | Chicago (Ill.)—Biography.

Classification: LCC F548.9.C5 W66 2024 (print) | LCC F548.9.C5 (ebook) | DDC 305.8951/073077311092 [B]—dc23/eng/20240222

LC record available at https://lccn.loc.gov/2024006057

LC ebook record available at https://lccn.loc.gov/2024006058

For C. W. Chan, Heidi Chan, Grace Chiu, Anna Ho, Iris Ho,
Paul Ho, Eleanor So, and David Wong
In memory of Bernarda "Bernie" Wong and Esther Wong

Contents

Foreword

Opening the storefront door of a Chicago Chinatown building was easy. . . . Getting up the stairs immediately in front of me looked harder. Sitting on nearly every step up to the second floor was a man with a child, a woman with a baby, a middle-aged couple, an elderly man. My camera crew and I struggled through all the people and made our way to an open door on the second floor. We came into a small room, dominated by a giant desk that filled most of the office space.

Standing near it was a tiny woman who smiled, put out her hand, and said, "Thank you so much for coming. I'm Bernie Wong."

Those nine words changed my life and began to form a blueprint for my career in Chicago. I had been a broadcast journalist for less than four years and had been in Chicago for only a year. Bernie Wong had called me at my television station and asked for help. A family of four, split between China and Chicago, was facing the mother's terminal cancer diagnosis here, while the father and young daughter were in China. Bernie had already learned it would take the intervention of someone in the federal government to get them to Chicago before the mother died. In limbo here was the family's twelve-year-old son.

Bernie Wong was a caring social worker, with a heart bigger than her barely five-foot-tall size. She, along with several other dedicated social workers, had seen the need for a community organization to help immigrants as well as Chinese American citizens. They had created the Chinese American Service League (CASL) just twenty-one months earlier. Seeing the crowd on the staircase told me plenty of residents were already coming for help. Bernie could not have known this case would teach her how she and the fledging agency could make a huge difference.

All we knew on this date in 1980 was that Mrs. So, who spoke no English, had collapsed at work and had been rushed to the hospital. When she regained consciousness, she could not explain to anyone that her little boy was sitting alone in an apartment in Chinatown. It took some time before hospital staff found CASL, a Chinese-speaking social worker, and finally, thanks to CASL staff, the frightened, hungry little boy.

Bernie Wong instinctively understood that the So family's story needed to be publicized and that attention might get some action from Washington, D.C. That is why she called me, the first Asian American journalist on a network station in Chicago. She hoped I would do a story. I did. You will learn the details of the So family story and the future of that little boy as you read this book.

In these early days, Bernie was a quiet woman who was motivated mostly by her mother's admonition to care for others. Bernie learned from this first major experience that all the calls she made, all the people she pressured to help, all the resources she discovered she could call on would help her become the fierce, dedicated, hardworking leader of CASL. As the years went by, I began to use the phrase "You can't say no to Bernie."

It is difficult to separate the story of Bernie Wong's life from the life, growth, and work of the CASL. But as the agency grew, it brought in many others who were dedicated to helping. And CASL sure did grow.

That small second-floor donated office space with the too-big donated desk began to spread into a room in another Chinatown building, a space donated by yet another building owner, and soon, there were scattered spaces all around Chinatown. So many needs also became apparent—from housing for brand-new immigrants, to childcare, to elder care, to after-school programs, to gang prevention, to teaching about social security, or Medicare, or starting small businesses. The needs popped up as quickly as people showed up at the various doorways (and stairs!) looking for help. When a large industrial garage space became available, Bernie set to work consolidating the scattered offices into one location.

Of course, first she had to get volunteers (including me) to convert the oily, greasy, cement garage into a usable office. Even as CASL moved into the garage, it was obvious the agency and the people it helped would keep on growing and would soon outgrow this space.

Bernie and her founding partners and the CASL board of directors knew that grants would not be enough to cover the needs of the agency. They approached me with the idea of forming an advisory board that would focus on fundraising to support CASL's programs. Bernie decided I would be the first head of the advisory board, and despite my busy, nearly seven-days-a-week work schedule, I "could not say no to Bernie."

It was through the work of the advisory board that I began to see how CASL's growing and changing clientele reflected the way the city of Chicago was changing. We recruited business leaders, philanthropists, local politicians, community workers, and other media folks to join our first advisory board. We put on at least two major fundraisers each year along with smaller functions. I had done very little of this kind of fundraising before and saw how Bernie tirelessly found people who could not say no to her. But all of the advisory board members were Asian. I began to see how most people, outside of the Asian community, believed in the "model minority" myth—that Asian immigrants and Asian American citizens did not need help, that we were all educated, had careers, were successful. Asian Americans were also a small, somewhat isolated portion of the local population. For many years, my phone calls and letters to potential donors stressed that although the Chinese community was invested in helping its own people, we also knew that each immigrant success story was helping to build Chicago economically and socially into a better city.

In the 1990s and definitely into the 2000s, CASL began to see Asian immigrants from places other than China or Hong Kong come for help. Soon, other ethnic groups in Chicago also began to come in to ask if they could enroll in some of CASL's job training programs. They were welcomed. At the same time, national and local statistics began to show that the fastest growing ethnic group in the United States and locally, by percentage, was Asian. Understanding began to grow that our community was becoming a bigger and bigger part of the fabric of Chicago.

We were able to recruit non-Asians onto the board.

I will always be grateful that ABC7, the television station I worked at for thirty-two years, was a huge supporter of community organizations and the agencies their anchor people believed in and supported. From the beginning of my involvement with CASL, Channel 7 strongly supported our CASL fundraisers.

Some years ago, I did research for an article I wrote about Chinatowns across the United States because a play about a Chinatown was about to open in Chicago. It was distressing to me to discover that every Chinatown in the United States was declining in population except one: Chicago's. As I searched for why, I came to believe a strong case can be made that the presence and growth of CASL played a major part in preserving and nurturing Chicago's Chinatown. This agency built a center that allowed the other community organizations, schools, churches, and politicians to gather. This agency built a large apartment building for seniors that kept them in the community where there was a hospital where their language was spoken and familiar foods were served. The agency's senior center allowed them to remain in a community of friends so that they did not feel isolated. The agency helped newcomers find local housing, and with the strength of the Chinatown population needs, new housing was built that allowed Chinatown to expand. Bernie Wong learned to speak up to politicians in Chicago and Springfield to gain support for CASL, and ultimately, that helped Chinatown.

I mentioned earlier that meeting Bernie changed my life. In 1980, with a Chicago career ahead of me, I was focused on the hard news I expected to cover. Already, I had learned that news and stories about real people were equally important. But as Bernie called on me more and more often (and I could not say no), I realized that my seat in front of the camera gave me entry through many doors and that my life off camera could be useful in helping others. It started me on the path of working not only with CASL but with many other charities in the city I love and call home.

More than anything, I think back to similarities in Bernie's life and mine. We started as shy, quiet individuals who became brave as we learned that we could do good in this world and help others. Each time we spoke up, pushed, or even demanded and made a positive difference for someone else, we got stronger. I am so grateful to have had a successful broadcasting career. But I am even more grateful that I did not say no and became a part of the work that has helped countless thousands of people over the years. An immigrant may have started as a small child in CASL's childcare program, which turned into getting an education, then starting in a profession, and having a family, or took a job training course that resulted in a job, which led to a business that provided jobs to many others.

Before she left us too soon, I was able to remind Bernie that she always reminisced about the hundreds of people who passed through CASL whom she helped. But she could never know the tens of thousands CASL continues to affect and influence. She did not have a huge ego and always pointed out the others who created CASL and stayed on for many years to work for the community. She married a man who liked to cook, but Albert soon excelled at it because Bernie was never home long enough to cook. Their only daughter, Shun, still thinks, without regret, that all the people at CASL were her siblings. Bernie wanted this book written, but she wanted it to be more about CASL than about her. My hope is that this book will be a guide and inspiration to the other Bernie Wongs to come who know their lives will be so meaningful because they have helped others.

Linda Yu
Chicago, Summer 2023

The Ten Founders of the
Chinese American Service League

This story would not have been possible without the insight and dedication of ten friends from Hong Kong who came together to help people less fortunate than themselves. Although their résumés are long and illustrious, these short biographies describe their backgrounds in the late 1970s when they founded CASL.

Bernarda "Bernie" Wong—Bernie was a graduate of Briar Cliff College in Sioux City, Iowa, and earned a master's in social work from Washington University in St. Louis. By 1978, she was employed as a social worker in East Chicago Heights, overseeing Head Start. She became the face of CASL, leading it for thirty-eight years. Bernie passed away in 2021.

Esther Wong—Esther was a graduate of the University of Hong Kong and worked as a social worker in Hong Kong before moving to Chicago to earn a master's in social work from the University of Chicago. A longtime CASL board member, she later worked as CASL's executive director alongside Bernie for almost twenty years. She was married to David Wong until she passed away in 2022.

David Wong—David was a graduate of Chung Chi College at the Chinese University of Hong Kong and earned a master's of theology degree from the Divinity School at the University of Chicago and a master's of education at Northwestern University. He worked for Chicago Public Schools as a coordinator of the Asian Resource Center for the Bilingual Program. He was married to Esther Wong until her death in 2022.

Anna Ho—Anna is a graduate of the University of California at Berkeley and taught in the Cantonese bilingual program at Senn High School in Chicago. She worked in youth programs when CASL was founded. She is married to Paul Ho.

Paul Ho—Paul Ho is a graduate of the University of California at Berkeley and was the librarian of the University of Chicago's East Asian Library. He met David Wong when he was a graduate student worker in the library. He designed the Chinese characters in the CASL logo and is married to Anna Ho.

C. W. Chan—C. W. Chan is a graduate of Chung Chi College at the Chinese University of Hong Kong and received a master's in social work from the University of Chicago. He was the head of psychiatric social work at Cook County Hospital. He served for many years as the CASL board president. He is married to Heidi Chan.

Heidi Chan—Heidi was a teacher in Hong Kong before studying pharmacy at the University of Illinois College of Medicine. She worked as a pharmacist at Loyola University and is married to C. W. Chan.

Eleanor So—Eleanor studied social work in Nelson, British Columbia. She taught English as a Second Language in Toronto before moving to Chicago. In Chicago, she taught English in Chinatown before CASL was founded. By 1978, she was working as a part-time receptionist in the dentistry of Dr. K. K. Wan.

Grace Chiu—Grace is a graduate of Chung Chi College at the Chinese University of Hong Kong and earned a PhD in sociology from the University of Chicago. She introduced Bernie and Albert Wong to other Hong Kong students at the University of Chicago.

Iris Ho—Iris is a graduate of Loyola University in Chicago. Grace Chiu introduced her to the group and met them for bowling at the University of Illinois at Chicago. She researched nonprofit funding at the public library and designed the CASL logo.

Author's Note

Chinese names are usually written surname first, followed by one or two given names. Because this story takes place in the United States and the CASL founders, staff, and clients have mostly either taken an English given name or have inverted their Chinese names to fit the American style, I have kept to their preferences and refer to them mainly with their given names first and surnames last.

Also, since there are only about fifty common Chinese surnames, I have decided to use a couple of different styles when referring to the CASL founders, staff, and clients. For the founders, since they came together to create a family community at CASL, I refer to them by their first or given names. I also usually refer to staff and clients by their first names to avoid confusion when several have the same surnames. But I have made the exception for staff who left CASL and became prominent leaders of other organizations—mostly in Chinatown—in which they still work. In these cases, I have used their surnames.

This book is the story of the Chinese American Service League, which cannot be told without telling Bernie Wong's story. Bernie was the only one among CASL's ten founders who stayed employed by the agency from its beginning until her retirement almost four decades later. During this time, Bernie became the face of CASL. Bernie's retirement and the onset of the pandemic seemed like a natural ending point for this book, so I end this work with events that took place in 2022. However, CASL's story continues today in broader and more ambitious ways that even the original founders could not have envisioned. These stories are yet to be told.

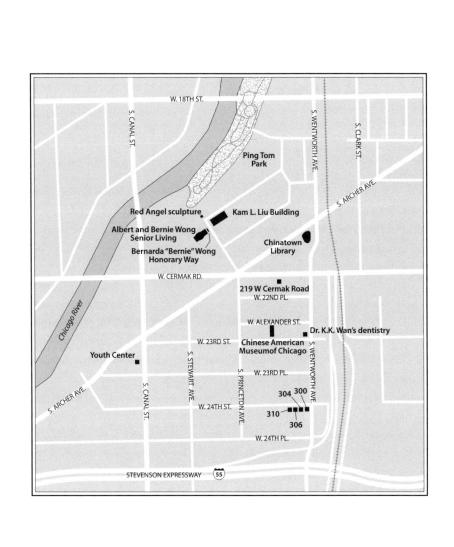

W. 18TH ST.

S. CANAL ST.

S. WENTWORTH AVE.

S. CLARK ST.

Ping Tom
Park

S. ARCHER AVE.

Red Angel sculpture

Kam L. Liu Building

Albert and Bernie Wong
Senior Living

Bernarda "Bernie" Wong
Honorary Way

Chinatown
Library

Chicago River

W. CERMAK RD.

219 W Cermak Road
W. 22ND PL.

W. ALEXANDER ST.

Dr. K.K. Wan's dentistry

W. 23RD ST.

Chinese American
Museum of Chicago

Youth Center

S. STEWART AVE.

S. PRINCETON AVE.

S. WENTWORTH AVE.

W. 23RD PL.

S. ARCHER AVE.

S. CANAL ST.

304 300

310

306

W. 24TH ST.

W. 24TH PL.

STEVENSON EXPRESSWAY 55

Prologue

Chinatown Diplomacy

It was a crisp autumn day in 1980 when So Yang Kun Yuk passed out at work. She had started her workday at a Chinatown restaurant the same as she had these last several months since immigrating from China with her twelve-year-old son, Herman. But ever since mother and son had arrived in Chicago on May 24 that year, a pesky cough seemed more of a nuisance to Mrs. So than a serious ailment. It certainly was not normal to faint at work.

Unresponsive at first, Mrs. So seemed confused and semiconscious as she came to, and her colleagues hastily called an ambulance. With a local Chinatown branch of the Chicago Fire Department not too far from the restaurant, paramedics arrived in no time. Mrs. So was taken to nearby Mercy Hospital, just east of Chinatown.

Mrs. So's husband, So Yee Kwong, and their daughter, Hanna, had stayed back in Guangzhou, where teenaged Hanna was a rising acrobatics star and Mr. So worked alongside her as a coach. The plan was for Mrs. So and Herman to gauge whether life in Chicago was truly worth uprooting the whole family. This was a time when Chinese acrobats served as the face of China around the world. Most Chinese citizens could not get visas to travel outside the country in 1980. And for those who were successful in receiving visas, the cost of overseas travel was prohibitively expensive as wages in China were then just a few hundred U.S. dollars a year. Touring acrobats comprised an elite group that flew to countries in the Eastern Bloc and beyond. Before China and most countries in the West had normalized diplomatic relations, acrobats served the same role as diplomats, performing before heads of state in cities like Beijing and Shanghai and on their overseas tours. The family felt it best for Mrs. So and Herman to first test the waters in Chicago before asking Hanna to give up such opportunities.

Now at the hospital, Mrs. So not only felt afraid that she was sick but worried terribly about twelve-year-old Herman, left alone at home in their Chinatown basement apartment. As a quiet boy who was still learning English, Herman dutifully waited in their apartment every day for his mother to return from work. Life in Chicago and the United States was still very new to both mother and son. When Herman realized she wasn't coming home, would he think she had gotten hurt or lost and couldn't find her way home? The possibilities were endless and they all pointed to nothing but fear and unease. Even worse, Mrs. So could not communicate with any of the nurses, doctors, or technicians at the hospital to let them know her young son was home alone and did not know she was in the hospital.

Mrs. So's mother tongue was Cantonese, and if any of the medical staff spoke a language besides English, it most likely would have been Spanish. The hospital staff hurried to find someone who could understand Cantonese—even a patient—so they could learn if she had family in the area. Doctors were still running tests on Mrs. So to learn why she had fainted when a hospital staff member suddenly remembered a name: Bernie Wong.

The staff member didn't know very much about Bernie except that she was Chinese, had an office in Chinatown, and helped people. The hospital administration set out to locate Bernie and figured there was a high probability that she would be able to communicate with Mrs. So.

Bernie was the executive director of the newly formed Chinese American Service League (CASL) on Cermak Road in Chinatown. Bernarda Wong, or "Bernie" to all who knew her, was an immigrant herself and had experienced what it was like to start over in a new country and a new city, especially one so different from Bernie's Hong Kong or the So family's Guangzhou. The hospital staff located Bernie's number at CASL and gave her a call.

As it turned out, Mrs. So and Herman may have already known Bernie. They certainly knew CASL. Soon after mother and son arrived in Chicago, they met with Bernie or another CASL staff member in the agency's second-floor office at 219 West Cermak, just steps from the Chinatown gate on Wentworth Avenue. Everyone in Chinatown knew of Bernie, so new immigrants usually found their way to her small office, up a steep flight of stairs.

In no time, Bernie arrived at Mercy and found Mrs. So alone and sapped of energy in a hospital bed. But as soon as Mrs. So saw Bernie walk through the door, her eyes lit up. Finally, there was someone who could understand her. Herman would be located and mother and son would soon reunite. Mrs. So had never felt so relieved to see another Chinese face. And sure enough, through Cantonese-English translation, Bernie informed the hospital staff that Mrs. So had a child at home.

Bernie also learned that Mrs. So's tests had finally come back and the diagnosis was unimaginable, especially for a new immigrant with a young son. Mrs. So had terminal lung cancer and wasn't expected to live another year. When Bernie heard this news, she felt called into action. Her mind started racing, just thinking about all that had to be done in a short amount of time. She knew she could rely on her staff and volunteers to ensure that Herman got to and from school and that he had enough to eat. Mrs. So would need help making and getting to her medical appointments.

Mrs. So was grateful for the help with her medical appointments and Herman's care, but she and Bernie both worried about the more pressing issue of how awful it would be if Mr. So and Hanna weren't able to come to Chicago before Mrs. So passed away. When the family parted earlier that year, they never imaged it would be for the last time. Bernie couldn't allow for that to happen, no matter how much time Mr. So and Hanna would have with Mrs. So. Plus, Bernie knew that Herman should not be left alone in his new country. However, it was anything but easy to arrange for a family reunion in the United States.

In 1980, the United States and China had resumed diplomatic relations only the previous year. Richard Nixon had taken his historic trip to China eight years earlier, but it wasn't until Jimmy Carter was in office in 1979 that the two countries officially recognized each other. For the previous thirty years, the United States had recognized the Republic of China (ROC), or Taiwan, as the sole legitimate Chinese state.

It would take a while for the People's Republic to establish embassies and consulates after not having had diplomatic relations with many countries since the end of the Chinese Civil War in 1949. The Chinese government opened a liaison office in Washington, D.C. in 1973 after the Nixon visit, which transitioned into an embassy once relations were formalized in 1979. But by the time Mrs. So had been diagnosed in late 1980, a Chinese consulate had yet to open in Chicago. That would not happen for several years, so Bernie did not have the luxury of appealing to a nearby Chinese consulate for help in reuniting the So family. Bernie was on her own to figure this out.

She would need to contact American politicians and others in positions of influence, turning to every connection she had made over the last couple of years at CASL and before that when she worked as a social worker in Chicago and in the low-income southern suburb of Ford Heights, then called East Chicago Heights. Locally, there was Mayor Jane Byrne. At the state level, she contacted Illinois governor Jim Thompson and at the federal levels, Senators Adlai Stevenson III and Charles Percy, as well as U.S. Representatives Cardiss Collins and Paul Simon.

"Bernie pulled strings to make the visit happen," Herman So recalled years later.

As she waited to hear from these politicians, Bernie figured out the correct paperwork to be filed in order to bring over Mr. So and Hanna from Guangzhou. Once that paperwork was submitted, months passed as Herman continued to go to school and Mrs. So's condition worsened. The wait felt like years, but finally, Bernie received the good news she had been waiting for: Mr. So's and Hanna's visa applications were approved. The So family would be reunited in Chicago in mid-1981.

Traveling from China to the United States in 1981 was not easy. The only airline that flew between the two countries was the Civil Aviation Administration of China, or CAAC as it was known. There certainly weren't direct flights to Chicago, so Mr. So and Hanna first flew to Los Angeles before connecting to a domestic flight. Bernie and Herman greeted them at O'Hare International Airport soon after they exited their plane.

The family came together in Chicago just months before Mrs. So passed away. She would not live to see 1982.

Left to right: So Yang Kun Yuk, Hanna So, and So Yee Kwong after CASL reunited the family in Chicago. Photo courtesy of Jacinta Wong.

The loss of Mrs. So was devastating to the family. Even though they knew that day would eventually arrive, it was still such a shock as no amount of preparation is ever enough. Bernie knew from her training and previous work in social services that immigrant children and children in poor families often assume adult roles when their parents are unable to spend adequate time attending to their families. She also understood the toll this took on both the children and parents, so it was with that understanding that she asked Mr. So if she could oversee Herman and Hanna's education, insisting Herman enroll at St. Therese School in Chinatown. As Bernie's mother had done for her, she wanted Herman to be educated at a private Catholic school. Bernie had a lifelong devotion to her Catholic faith and went on to attend St. Therese every Sunday, no matter her current work challenge or plans for future ones. Bernie would often recruit new staff members from St. Therese and would bring other staff to church if they showed any inclination for attending.

Hanna was already a teenager and the age to attend high school, so Bernie was determined she attend one with bilingual services. St. Therese only had a K–8 school, so that wasn't an option for students after they finished eighth grade.

Chinatown did not have a public high school. Most teens in Chinatown instead traveled ten miles north to Senn High School, which had a bilingual Cantonese program to help with the influx of Vietnamese refugees, the majority of which were Cantonese speakers. Hanna needed these bilingual services and enrolled at Senn. Anna Ho, another CASL founder, had participated in a bilingual teaching program at Northwestern University and went on to teach at Senn. She got to know Hanna well and recruited her for the school's international night. Hanna performed a floor acrobatics routine to represent her bilingual class. "Hanna was such a great acrobat and was super flexible," Anna recalled. "So everyone was very impressed."

Bernie also hoped Hanna could keep up her acrobatics in Chicago, even though she had left her troupe back in China. Since CASL had no extra funding and Bernie believed that the budget should be spent on programs for clients, she had to rely on donations when putting together fundraisers. When CASL hosted a fundraising dinner at the Chiam Restaurant on Wentworth, Bernie recruited Hanna to perform an acrobatics routine as part of the entertainment for the evening.

Bernie's daughter, Shun, or Jacinta as her parents and friends called her, became involved with CASL from an early age and assisted with these performances. "I helped Hanna with her equipment for a year or two while I was still in grammar school," Jacinta recalled. People would always tease Jacinta that CASL was her sibling because Bernie never had time to have more children, as she was too busy raising CASL.

| | |

When it came time for Herman to attend high school, Bernie felt he could use his academic success at St. Therese and apply to a Catholic school closer to home. His need for bilingual services were long behind him. With guidance from Bernie and other staff at CASL, Herman applied to and was accepted at the prestigious De La Salle, not too far from Chinatown. Five Chicago mayors had graduated from De La Salle at that time, including father and son Richard J. and Richard M. Daley.

To prepare for life in the United States, Mr. So received job counseling at CASL. But he had always had a sense of adventure and wanted to see more of the United States. With his children in high school, he traveled around the country seeking work, leaving Herman and Hanna to look out for themselves in Chinatown. "My dad would call us once a week when we were in school," Herman recalled. Bernie often checked in with them, too.

After Hanna finished high school, she and her father settled in Orlando, where they both became restaurateurs. Herman, the quiet boy who had faced the dire possibility of being orphaned in Chicago if Bernie hadn't fought with all she had to bring his father and sister to Chicago, went on to become valedictorian of his 1988 De La Salle class. Herman was also a star soccer player in high school and volunteered as a tutor at CASL, giving back to the agency that had given him so much hope and encouragement.

Left to right: Hanna So, Bernie, So Yee Kwong, and Herman So after Bernie reunited Herman with his sister and father. Photo courtesy of Jacinta Wong.

Early in his senior year of high school, Herman was accepted at the University of Illinois. The U of I now had the second largest academic library in the country behind Harvard and would have provided Herman with an excellent education. "But my high school chemistry teacher and soccer coach encouraged me to apply to the United States Air Force Academy," Herman recalled. "They were looking for soccer players and my teacher recommended me." Herman's teacher and coach was impressed with both his athleticism and academic strength.

And sure enough, Herman's hard work paid off and the Air Force Academy accepted him. "Those were the toughest four years of my life," Herman said. Still, he made a career in the air force for two decades and retired as a captain in 2001. He's now a successful consumer product marketing executive. Herman met his wife, Sherry, during their school years at St. Therese, and they are now the proud parents of four grown children, each excelling in their chosen fields of engineering, psychology, and marketing.

With the guidance and compassion of Bernie Wong and the staff and volunteers at CASL, Herman found a home in Chicago and went on to live the American dream in ways most people in the United States could only dream of. His story is just like those of Bernie Wong and the other nine CASL founders. They settled in Chicago and went on to provide services to children, senior citizens, and all ages in between by establishing programs, counseling services, and housing. In doing so, they helped shape Chinatown, Chicago, and the United States. These stories are as American as apple pie.

PART I

The Early Years in the 1970s

1

Hong Kong Connections

Bernie Wong was born in Hong Kong in 1943, but her story begins in South America. Her mother, Virginia Chia, was born and raised in Huacho, Peru, to a father named Carlos Chia, who had come from China to run a shipping business in South America, and a mother named Cristina Salinas who was half-Chinese and half-Basque and relished her role as a socialite more than that of a mother. Virginia's parents split up while she was still a young girl, after Cristina discovered that Carlos had another wife and family back in China. Cristina kicked him out and had their marriage annulled.

Carlos decided to go back to Zhongshan in Guangdong Province, never to return to Peru. But even after the break from her husband, Cristina wasn't keen on parenting. An uncle in Lima who believed in girls' education happily took in young Virginia, making sure she attended school. Virginia also entered the Miss Chinatown pageants in Lima and went on to enjoy her teenage years, despite the abandonment by her parents.

Growing up, Virginia wanted to be a nun and entered a convent in the Philippines, only to be kicked out several times. Her sense of humor and her love of dancing and eating did not win her any favors from the strict nuns. Bernie's daughter, Jacinta, remembers her grandmother Virginia dancing around the family living room in Chicago. "She would sing in Spanish and balance fruit on her head like the actor and dancer Carmen Miranda."

Back in Peru, Virginia met her husband after he traveled to South America from China on business when he was a teenager, apprenticing to take over his father's successful cotton farm. Virginia's husband's surname was Lo, and because he was spending so much time in Peru, he took the given name of Jorge José. The couple dated for five years before marrying in Peru at a time when many Chinese couples entered arranged marriages. Virginia and Jorge chose to follow their hearts.

They traveled to Hong Kong for their honeymoon in the 1930s, but the British colony was not yet the sprawling metropolis it is today. Virginia appreciated Hong Kong's mixture of East and West because it reminded her of the Chinese communities of Peru. She preferred to wear Western dresses and not the Chinese cheongsam that women wore in China at that time, so she felt at home in Hong Kong because it was just as acceptable to wear Western fashion there as it was to wear Chinese styles. Virginia spoke Spanish as her mother tongue and English with a slight Spanish accent but didn't speak any Chinese dialects.

Since Virginia was estranged from her mother and no longer had contact with her father, there was nothing keeping her in Peru. She was close to the uncle, aunt, and cousins who had raised her, but Jorge was now her family and she was happy to follow him to Hong Kong for his business.

The couple would not stay long in Hong Kong in the 1930s because Jorge felt his business opportunities were greater in southern China. So they left Hong Kong and moved just over the border to the Chinese city of Shiqi in the Zhongshan District. Jorge's business soon thrived between southern China and Hong Kong, so he, Virginia, and their growing number of children ended up splitting their time between both cities.

Yet war on many fronts plagued China during the 1930s and 1940s. The Japanese military had started taking parts of northeast China at the same time the Nationalist government battled a civil war with the Communist opposition. Virginia and Jorge sent their five sons to a Chinese village, which was supposed to be safer than the cities in China since the Japanese usually bombed only the cities. They took their oldest daughter to Hong Kong, and their second daughter, Bernie, was born in Hong Kong in 1943 as war raged across the British colony and China. Food was scarce and it was difficult to find protein-rich ingredients, so Bernie subsisted mainly on cornstarch as an infant.

The family returned to Guangzhou after World War II ended, but their stable lives lasted only a few short years. World War II ended for the rest of the world in 1945, but China could not enjoy peace as its civil war between the Nationalists and Communists flared up again. At that point, Jorge was selling clothing in flea markets as well as operating a bakery and café, while Virginia made a living as a successful seamstress and sewing teacher. Jorge opened a hotel, which became his last business venture in China until news got around that the winning Communists had started to confiscate property. Many business owners, small and large, decided to flee China for the safety of British Hong Kong or the island of Taiwan.

Bernie, her sister, and their youngest brother were sent to the Portuguese colony of Macau to live with an aunt while one brother was sent to Hong Kong with a family friend. Virginia soon joined three of her children in Macau—a forty-mile trip over the South China Sea—while Jorge stayed back in Guangzhou along with their two oldest sons to take care of business until Communist soldiers marched into the city.

Just a day before the Los were to leave Guangzhou, Jorge suffered an accident when a bicycle handle cut him near his throat. Medical attention was almost impossible to find, as the city was about to be taken by the Communists. Jorge decided it was time to give up his business in Guangzhou and took his two sons, miraculously finding passage for the three of them on the last ship to Hong Kong.

The Lo family was not new to Hong Kong, but they did not have it easy. Jobs were nonexistent, especially for people who could not speak English like Jorge. He was still incapacitated from his injury, and all the family and business possessions were left behind in Guangzhou with no way to get them back. While Jorge tried to settle back into Hong Kong, Virginia found work at a department store in tailoring and alterations. She was soon able to open her own tailoring business while Jorge managed the books and the household chores. Bernie saw in her mother a strong woman who took charge of her family, all to provide for her seven children and her husband. Virginia even found extra work tutoring Spanish, working late into the evenings.

Catholicism was very important to Virginia, and when a number of nuns were detained by the police for "wearing strange clothes," Virginia went down to the police station to arrange for their release. Back when Jorge still ran his hotel, which stood across from the Kowloon-Canton Railway station in Guangzhou, he and Virginia would also help priests and nuns passing through the city, offering free accommodations and food at their hotel and restaurant. When the Lo family settled in Hong Kong for good, Virginia was able to enroll all of her children in prestigious Catholic schools in gratitude for all her help. In 1949, Bernie started at Saint Mary's Canossian College, a girls' high school on the Kowloon peninsula. Hong Kong used the British educational system and primary and secondary schools were often called colleges.

Like many refugee families in Hong Kong at the time, the Lo family of nine rented one small room in an apartment unit. There wasn't enough room for the whole family to sleep in this one room, so Bernie's five brothers spread out newspapers on the floor in the hall, creating a makeshift bed and covering themselves in blankets to keep warm during Hong Kong's damp and cooler months. The other rooms in the apartment unit were occupied with other, unrelated people.

This type of living arrangement—cramming several families into one apartment unit meant for one family—was common in Hong Kong for decades.

Virginia would take her children to help out at soup kitchens and other community-based organizations in Hong Kong. Bernie fondly recalled her mother's passion for giving back. "My mother, on her own, was a social worker. She had people knocking on our door needing some help, whether it's food, whether it's training, whether it's counseling. So I grew up watching my mom do a lot of social work from home."[1]

As difficult as their lives felt in war-torn China and later in Hong Kong, Virginia taught her kids that there were always others who had it worse. Bernie was named, after all, from the patron saint of the ill and poor.

This was also a time when the Hong Kong government did not provide much in terms of social welfare, despite a growing refugee population from mainland China. In fact, the population of Hong Kong would increase exponentially from Bernie's early childhood to the time she graduated high school, all with minimal resources. It took a hillside fire in 1953 that displaced more than fifty thousand residents for the British colonial government to embrace the concept of public housing. Other social services were all but nonexistent. This was the Hong Kong Bernie grew up in. Virginia's guidance to help others would have a profound impact on Bernie in her adult years.

| | |

As the youngest in the family, Bernie was her parents' favorite. It wasn't easy to succeed at school, as the exams were bilingual in English and Chinese and very competitive. "Every year students committed suicide due to the pressures of the exams," Bernie recalled.[2] They often feared losing face, or the shame of humiliation, for their families if they did not pass their exams.

Students could choose instruction in either English or Cantonese, although they would have to take the other as their second language. Bernie chose the English track and excelled in all of her classes except for Chinese. She was able to earn money by tutoring other students in English and in subjects that did not involve written Chinese. "My level of Chinese was only at a sixth grade level," she said.[3]

By the time Bernie was to graduate high school at the age of eighteen, she desired more than anything to study social work in the United States. She wanted to follow in her mother's footsteps when it came to helping others. Going abroad was not a new concept for the Lo family. "By the time I graduated high school, only two of my brothers were left in Hong Kong. Most came to the U.S. to go to college," Bernie said.[4] Her older sister had already settled in Canada for marriage and was living in British Columbia. Bernie started campaigning her parents to allow her to apply to schools in the United States. She also had a valid reason: in the early 1960s, Hong Kong had only one university—the University of Hong Kong—and competition for acceptance was extremely difficult. A year or two after Bernie started college, another university would open—the Chinese University of Hong Kong—but by that time, Bernie had already settled into college life in the United States.

Virginia agreed to let Bernie apply to college outside Hong Kong but gave her three conditions. First, Virginia insisted Bernie continue her Catholic education. There were many Catholic colleges and universities in the United States, so Bernie didn't see that as a problem. Second, Bernie could only apply to all-women schools. Again, at that time, there were many women's colleges in the United States that enjoyed a solid academic reputation. This requirement would also not be difficult to fulfill. Finally, this Catholic, all-female school would need to be located in a rural area, far from any big city. Virginia wanted her youngest daughter away from the vices of big cities.

Bernie researched her options, looking through a college catalog arranged alphabetically. When she reached the Bs, she found that Briar Cliff College in Sioux City, Iowa, fit her mother's criteria. It was a Catholic women's school 480 miles from Chicago and 270 miles from Minneapolis. Bernie would be securely tucked away in the cornfields of Iowa. She applied to Briar Cliff and won a full, four-year scholarship, including room and board.

Getting to the United States should have been easy at that point, as Bernie proved she would not be a burden to the state since she had earned a full ride, including living expenses. But in the early 1960s, all travelers arriving into the United States from Hong Kong had to show a clear X-ray free from any respiratory issues, especially tuberculosis. When Bernie went for the requisite X-ray, the scan showed a dark spot on her left lung. This was shockingly bad news and could prevent her from a college education in the United States. She had no symptoms or any inclination she suffered from a disease like tuberculosis, so she figured a second opinion might be worthwhile.

"My cousin was a nurse," Bernie recollected, "and told me to take another X-ray. That was clear."[5] But when she took this second scan to the U.S. consulate in Hong Kong, the visa officer wouldn't accept it. Virginia stepped in and took Bernie to a Catholic hospital for a third scan, hoping it would come out as clear as the second. Yet this time, a spot appeared in her right lung. Bernie could not get a break.

Since the second scan was clear and because those two problematic scans each showed a spot in a different lung, Bernie didn't think there would be any harm in going back to the U.S. consulate and telling them the truth. The visa officer listened closely and empathized with her frustration, signing off on Bernie's application.

But her elation was short lived. The visa officer then informed Bernie that the U.S. government had just enacted a new policy for foreign students entering America. Instead of immediately starting their degree programs of study, foreign students would now need to complete one year of preparatory education. Bernie knew she didn't need to prepare for college in the United States since her entire education had been instructed in English. But rules are rules, and Virginia saw a way to make this work. "My mom suggested I apply to college in Canada where my sister now lived. I was accepted by one college that offered me a tuition scholarship, but no room and board. I knew this wasn't enough," Bernie said.[6] The family could not afford these expenses, even with Bernie living with her sister and brother-in-law. An extra mouth to feed would pose a difficult problem.

Around the time Bernie received her admittance letter from the Canadian school, she also learned that a friend in Hong Kong was headed to the U.S. consulate since he, too, was bound for America to study. Bernie told him about her predicament. He listened and suggested she come along to his appointment with the vice-consul. There was always a chance she could get an exemption from this preparatory year since her English was fluent and she had already studied in an English track for more than a decade.

So the two friends headed to the U.S. consulate on Hong Kong Island, and as soon as Bernie mentioned Briar Cliff, the vice-consul's eyes lit up. He was from Iowa and was delighted to hear Bernie was headed to his home state. He didn't think Bernie should waste any more time before starting college, so he signed her

Bernie Wong with her parents, Virginia and Jorge Lo. Photo courtesy of Jacinta Wong.

papers right there so she could bypass this preparatory year and enter Briar Cliff as planned that coming academic year. Eighteen-year-old Bernie was finally headed to the United States.

| | |

Virginia was pleased about her youngest daughter's education plans, yet still worried about sending Bernie to the middle of America. Iowa, after all, was a part of the United States that saw winters much unlike the mild ones in Hong Kong. Each year, Hong Kong temperatures could drop to a few degrees Celsius above freezing but would never dip below the zero mark. Indoor heating was a rarity in homes, but people managed with another layer or two of long underwear along with rubber hot water bottles they could place in their beds or under sweaters or jackets. Iowa was known for frigid winters with snow, strong wind, ice, and temperatures well below freezing. Virginia couldn't let Bernie leave for the United States without sending her off with proper clothing for these conditions.

Putting her seamstress skills to use, Virginia tailored not just one but seven warm coats for Bernie. When she finished the coats and it was time for Bernie to pack for her long journey, the two women stuffed each pair of coat arms into those of another coat and repeated this until all seven formed one solid form. Since the coats were Bernie's most valuable possession at this point, Virginia made sure Bernie carried these coats onto her flights. There certainly wasn't room in her stuffed suitcases and it would cost a fortune to pay for extra luggage.

Bernie's coats were so stiff, packed one into the other, that they appeared as a mannequin. She carried this bulk with one hand around the coats' waist and held her typewriter in the other. She also needed to bring her X-rays in her carry-on baggage. "At that time, that was the policy," Bernie remembered. "You needed to carry your X-rays with you so that when you entered the country, they could look at that."[7] As she boarded the plane with all of these belongings, "I looked like Dorothy in *The Wizard of Oz* getting on that plane."

There were no direct flights from Hong Kong to Iowa or even to Chicago for that matter, so Bernie's trip to the United States involved multiple legs, including Tokyo, Seattle, and Los Angeles. But she didn't have to travel the whole distance on her own, as the friend who took her to the U.S. consulate was also on her flights until they reached Seattle. Yet changing planes in Seattle without the help of this friend proved more harrowing than Bernie expected. "I thought at the time that people would help you along but they didn't. I ran like mad to catch that one flight, not knowing the direction and was holding my seven coats and everything!"[8]

Bernie flew on to Los Angeles, where she stayed with one of her brothers for a week before flying to Sioux City. "I remember it was a very small plane and it was early in the morning. The flight attendant gave me a cup of tea. I put my cup of tea on [the] tray table, turned around and got something, and the tea just slid down because the plane was on a slant and tea got all over my skirt. I was already anxious and nervous and now I was all wet. What a way to land!"[9]

When Bernie finally arrived at Briar Cliff College, she was one of only a few Asian students. "I was very shy at the time and couldn't catch all the English," Bernie recalled. "People spoke very fast and the American accent was very different."[10] Since Hong Kong at that time had been a British colony for 120 years, Bernie had learned English with a British accent, not an American one.

Due to homesickness and this language barrier, Bernie's first year in Iowa was lonely and difficult. "There was another Chinese girl in the college who was already a senior. She had graduated from the same high school in Hong Kong and happened to be a friend of my sister."

The white students were nice to Bernie, but she did not feel like she was one of them because of some cultural differences that became a big issue that first year. "I remember one day I brought out one of those Chinese embroidered bedspreads for my bed. And when I came back from the library, my roommate had swept the floor. Instead of putting the broom and dustpan back, she just lay them on my bed and I was very upset. I couldn't figure out why. Things like this should belong on the floor and not on the bed, but nobody else thought much of it," Bernie remembered.[11]

Even though Bernie was used to cramped conditions in Hong Kong, she found it challenging living among so many people. Her freshman dorm room housed six students, so it was often very noisy, especially since the others couldn't study without the radio on. "I was used to a quiet home and when I study I want something quiet," she recalled.[12] She also had a tough first year because she arrived on campus with only $80. Most of this money ended up going to the postage stamps for the many letters she wrote home, yet Bernie never asked her family for money. But she did tell her sister in Canada that she was hungry.

Each night during her first year, Bernie stayed up studying past midnight and sometimes went to bed hungry because she had missed the college's five o'clock dinnertime. After telling her sister that she wasn't eating enough, her sister and brother-in-law in Canada sent her dried noodles and canned food from the grocery store they owned.

Her sophomore year would change with the arrival of her childhood friend, Rosaline Lee. Now with a familiar face around—and one to room with—Bernie acclimated to the United States much better. The two friends enjoyed many adventures in college. Rosaline, now Rosaline Fung, recalled a costume party they attended their sophomore year.

Bernie on the left with her friend Rosaline Lee Fung, dressed as Audrey Hepburn at Briar Cliff College in Sioux City, Iowa. Photo courtesy of Jacinta Wong.

Bernie and I were hardworking roommates, trying to save enough from our baby-sitting jobs to go see the New York World's Fair that summer. We made sacrifices by cutting out all our weekend activities except once when we wanted to attend a masquerade party. But alas, we had no budget for our costumes. Inspired by the ads of *Breakfast at Tiffany's*, Bernie decided we should go to the party as twins, looking like Holly Golightly in the movie. You must remember we lived in an era when all young girls wanted to look like Audrey Hepburn. Dorm rooms were plastered with posters of the Holly Golightly character advertising the movie—Audrey Hepburn in a sleek black dress showing off bony arms. So Bernie started to get us ready for the party. By the time she finished with our hair, all piled up on top of our heads, no one could miss our Audrey Hepburn look.

We had a wonderful time that evening, but it was not until weeks afterwards that we really had a good laugh. Ironically, when we finally got to see the movie, we learned that Holly Golightly was a high-class call girl, definitely not someone that good Catholic girls would want to emulate. So Bernie's intentions of being sophisticated and beautiful for a night got us a good laugh and a good story to tell for years to come.[13]

Bernie was a great friend to Rosaline and asked the nuns at Briar Cliff for special permission to cook Chinese food for dinner one night. Rosaline was homesick for the food she missed back in Hong Kong, and from this gracious gesture from her friend, she could see that Bernie put others first and would do whatever she could to make them feel at home. This outlook would inspire Bernie to study social work at the graduate level after earning her bachelor's degree in sociology in 1966. She went on to the Brown School at Washington University in St. Louis to earn a master's in social work. But it wouldn't be too long before she would make her way to Chicago.

| | |

When Bernie arrived in the United States, the second wave of the feminist movement had just started. Her time at Briar Cliff and later in graduate school at Washington University in St. Louis made a big impression on her. Bernie's mother also played a guiding role in her views on feminism, as did the changes in the United States. Bernie spoke about this in a 1982 interview for a research project about Chinese American women. "I like to see women being able to pursue whatever they want to pursue, especially in terms of career. I think Women's Liberation has enabled women to do that. It has also changed a lot of men's ideas in terms of women's roles. I think it has helped men to recognize their own role too in terms of how men see themselves as partners more so now . . . since we both do pretty much the same thing."[14]

But at that point, Bernie was not as politically involved as she would become in the future.

In 1966, after Bernie's graduation from Briar Cliff and before she started graduate school at Washington University, she found a summer job in Chicago and lived with her brother Albert. A college student in Missouri, Albert Lo spent his summers working as a waiter in Chicago and shared a one-bedroom apartment with nine other Hong Kong students over a flower shop on Cermak Road in Chinatown. Some slept in the bedroom, while others found space in the living room. Bernie was friendly with some of Albert's roommates, and it was while in Chicago that she met another Albert—a graduate student in physics at the University of Chicago—and started dating him. Bernie and Albert Wong would have a long-distance relationship while she was in St. Louis until they married in 1968.

With a master's degree and now named Bernie Wong, she found a job with the Illinois Department of Children and Family Services on Damen and Taylor near Cook County Hospital. For a couple of years, Bernie worked on adoption cases before overseeing the Head Start program in a suburb that was then called

Bernie at her 1966 college graduation from Briar Cliff College in Sioux City, Iowa with her parents, Jorge and Virginia Lo, and her brother, George Lo. Photo courtesy of Jacinta Wong.

East Chicago Heights (now Ford Heights), one of the poorest communities in the country. Yet these challenges did not deter Bernie and her efforts paid off. She was soon promoted to director of social services. Besides working with children's programs, she also ran nutrition programs for senior citizens, a food pantry, and a homemaker program.

By the early 1970s, Bernie felt at home in Chicago with Albert and their baby daughter, Jacinta. With a fulfilling job, she also found a close-knit social circle, thanks to her husband and his friends at the University of Chicago. They enjoyed gathering for potluck dinners on the weekends and going on outings to bowling alleys. Sometimes they played board games like Risk until one o'clock in the morning.

Bernie fit in perfectly as these friends all came from Hong Kong. At that time in Chicago, there wasn't a large community of professionals and graduate students

Bernie and Albert with their infant daughter, Jacinta, in March 1972.
Photo courtesy of Jacinta Wong.

from Hong Kong. The 1965 Immigration Act was still relatively new and was a
significant turning point in U.S. immigration law. It lifted the immigration quotas
from the National Origins Act of 1924 that stopped immigration from Asia, barred
Chinese women from joining their husbands in the United States, and stripped the
citizenship of American citizens if they married Chinese men. The 1924 act came
after the already prohibitive 1882 Chinese Exclusion Act, which banned Chinese
laborers and their wives from immigrating to the United States.

Just as the United States started opening immigration from Asia in the mid-
1960s, China was just going into the Cultural Revolution, a frenzied time of
children turning in parents for being enemies of the state and students turning
in teachers for siding with Western intellectualism. Schools closed and teenagers
were sent to the countryside to learn from the peasants. It was all but impossible
for Chinese citizens to emigrate. For these reasons, most of the new Chinese
immigrants who settled in Chicago in the 1960s came from other places in the
diaspora like Hong Kong or Taiwan.

| | |

The friends from Hong Kong first gathered together thanks to Grace Chiu, a sociology doctoral student at the University of Chicago. Her husband played bridge and Ping-Pong with Albert Wong at the U of C, but Grace had already known some of these friends since many were graduates of Chung Chi College at the Chinese University of Hong Kong. They came to the United States to attend graduate school at the University of Chicago, and many of them spent time at International House, a residential building on campus that brought together students from around the world to foster greater cultural understanding.

One of Grace's most lasting introductions occurred when she introduced Bernie to another University of Chicago graduate student named Esther Wong. Esther was studying social work at the University of Chicago and had received her undergraduate degree from the University of Hong Kong. At this time, Esther's husband, David, was in the Divinity School, also at the University of Chicago, and had graduated with a bachelor's degree from the Chinese University of Hong Kong. This meeting would prove to be auspicious and life-changing.

As these friends started to get together regularly, along with Anna and Paul Ho, C. W. and Heidi Chan, and Eleanor So—all from Hong Kong—they would speak of their new lives in Chicago. Besides Bernie and Esther, C. W. and Eleanor also had backgrounds in social work. C. W. was the head of psychiatric social work at Cook County Hospital, and Eleanor had studied social work in Canada before moving to Chicago.

By the mid-1970s, Eleanor had found volunteer work teaching English as a Second Language (ESL) to adult students in a rented driving school space in Chinatown. These ESL classes provided new immigrants and senior citizens with language skills that would help them adjust to life in Chicago; the courses were also a means to socialize and express their frustrations and wishes when it came to living in Chicago, namely in Chinatown.

With her social work background, Eleanor was a sympathetic listener and reported her experiences back to her resourceful friends from Hong Kong. Together, they were about to change Chinatown and Chicago in ways none of them could ever have dreamed.

2

Eleanor So and Her Seniors

Eleanor So left Hong Kong to study in Canada and married there several years before she arrived in Illinois in 1975. Thanks to her husband, she had connections to the University of Chicago community, including the other CASL founders. Her husband had been a graduate student of the university and had also lived in International House.

"I had a social work degree from Nelson, British Columbia, but it was difficult to understand people in Canada at first even though I had gone to English-speaking convent schools in Hong Kong," Eleanor recalled. From this experience, she knew how it felt to move to another country and not understand people on the street. As with Bernie, Eleanor also grew up listening to British-accented English. Canadian English accents, much like the Chicago ones, were different and it took some adjusting before Eleanor could fully understand people in Nelson. By the time she moved to Chicago, North American accents posed no difficulty, but her memories of her initial hardships remained.

To occupy her time alone while her husband worked full time, Eleanor decided to volunteer in Chicago's Chinatown. "I had taught ESL in Toronto before moving to Chicago," Eleanor recounted. In her new home in Chicago, she figured she could help new immigrants learn English and perhaps assist some long-term residents with English, too. She learned that English instructional classes were being held in a rented space at a Chinatown driving school office. Eleanor was able to volunteer there and quickly understood that the need for English classes was much greater than she first imagined. She also realized that many elderly residents had never left the boundaries of Chinatown. They couldn't understand enough English to read the street signs, but they also didn't feel confident to venture downtown or to walk along Lake Michigan, one of Chicago's greatest treasures.

Eleanor's students mostly spoke Cantonese, so she could communicate with them without problem. The students were a combination of new immigrants and senior citizens, and whereas the younger classmates usually rushed off to work after their morning class, the older students enjoyed sticking around to speak more with Eleanor. Through these conversations she learned they needed more help than just lessons in conversational English. "My students were new immigrants who worked in restaurants or dry cleaners and had language barriers," she remembered, "for instance, when it came to going to the Social Security Agency. They also could not communicate when they tried to apply for their families to come from Hong Kong or China. It was impossible to fill out the forms."

Without someone to help them—preferably someone bilingual—it was nearly impossible for these students to enjoy the normal life of a Chicago resident. Eleanor offered to stay after class to help her students fill out these forms. But word got out around the community, and soon she had so many requests that she had no time to eat lunch. She couldn't keep up even if she worked without a break until her husband ended his workday.

She also learned about other issues. An older man in her class lived in a Chinatown rooming house and rarely left the confines of Wentworth and Cermak. With no relatives in the area, he had not kept up with regular, preventative medical checkups. It was so difficult for people in Chinatown to find doctors and dentists when they were accustomed to only working and sleeping. Eleanor helped this elderly man schedule an appointment with a doctor and accompanied him there.

Another student felt trapped at home while her husband worked long hours. She was fifty-seven years old and relatively new to Chicago, but her husband had lived in Chicago for decades and couldn't grasp her loneliness. He had never experienced that himself. She had no friends and ended up crying during the day while her husband was at work. "When someone called their home," Eleanor recalled, "she would always have her husband answer."

When she learned about Eleanor's English class, she quickly enrolled just to have a reason to get out of the house. She also figured she could learn some basic English in case someone called on the phone during the day while her husband was at work.

Eleanor's class turned out to be so much more than this woman expected. It gave her skills and confidence so that after a while, she insisted on answering the phone even when her husband was home. She learned to enjoy speaking English and took great pride in the progress she had made in Eleanor's class. Most of all, she connected with Eleanor, another Chinese immigrant like herself who had also learned English as a second language.

For the two to three years that Eleanor taught English, she typically had about twenty students in each class. Besides providing them with the skills to make medical appointments and answer the phone, Eleanor realized her students needed some fun in their lives. It was important to take care of basic necessities, but there was no reason her students couldn't also do things simply for joy. For this, Eleanor devised her most ambitious plan yet. She would teach her students how to travel outside of Chinatown.

Mrs. Yu was in her sixties and had a daughter in the suburbs whom she wished to visit more often but felt unable to leave Chinatown. Like many Chinatown senior citizens, she did not want to become a burden to her family and felt she couldn't ask her daughter to drive into the city more than a few times a month. "She could only see her daughter when the daughter picked her up," Eleanor remembered.

When Eleanor learned about Mrs. Yu's concerns, she devised a plan to help her travel beyond Chinatown with the confidence of the Chicagoans who made this trip every day. The route on public transportation to Mrs. Yu's daughter's home involved more than one Chicago Transit Authority (CTA) train line, so it was important for her to understand where to transfer and which train to board at the interchange. Mrs. Yu gained the self-assurance not only to travel to her daughter's home, but when friends from China or other parts of North America visited her in Chicago, Mrs. Yu happily took the "L" (elevated train) out to O'Hare to greet them at their airport gate once that train line connected to the airport in the mid-1980s. This was before 9/11 when it was still possible for people to go right to the gate to meet or send off family and friends.

Eleanor motivated her students to learn public transportation routes not just by reading English signs but also by having them ask the driver or conductor for directions. Many of her senior citizen students did not have a job waiting for them after their English class, so Eleanor would use this free time to take around ten students on city buses to places like the fabled Museum of Science and Industry in Chicago's Hyde Park neighborhood.

As her students were about to board a southbound bus, Eleanor would suddenly pretend as if she didn't know them. "I had them ask the bus driver to tell them when they reached their stop," she recalled. It was also up to the students to pay their own fares. Eleanor boarded after them, just in case any of the seniors needed help. Yet the ride to the museum was not just an exercise in taking public transportation. Eleanor guided them into the museum, where they would spend a carefree afternoon among the old airplanes, trains, and hatching baby chicks in a see-through incubator.

If the students did well with this public transportation exercise, which inevitably was the case, Eleanor would reward them with a trip to the Playboy Club off North Michigan Avenue, the first of two dozen nightclubs with waitresses wearing corseted costumes with cotton tails and bunny ears. Chicago in the mid-to-late 1970s was not what it is today. There was no Millennium Park or pedestrian-friendly Museum Campus. The Loop was gritty with only a few big department stores as a draw. Landmarks like the Sears Tower and Water Tower Place were brand new. The Playboy Club seemed like the most American place Eleanor could think of, both with its over-the-top waitresses dressed as corseted bunnies and headline acts like Barbra Streisand and Aretha Franklin. It felt like a world away from Chinatown.

Yet these outings were also learning experiences. "They had to order drinks themselves in English and chose things like Singapore Slings," Eleanor said. "But sometimes they would fall back on the Chinese pronunciation and we would all have a good laugh." Outings to the Playboy Club were probably the most fun her class had outside Chinatown.

| | | |

Eleanor and her husband lived in a high-rise apartment building in Hyde Park. Anna and Paul Ho lived on the same floor. Also in that building were Esther and David Wong and Heidi and C. W. Chan. David and Paul had also started volunteer teaching ESL in Chinatown, and when the group of friends met up, along with Bernie and Albert Wong and Grace Chiu and her husband, their conversations would often turn to the community, which had been in Chicago for more than one hundred years at that point.

Eleanor regaled her friends with stories of the never-ending forms to be filled out. "I asked them to help because there was too much work for one person," she said. She also told them of her outings with Chinatown residents. From these conversations, another idea came to Eleanor. "I spoke with C. W., Bernie, and Esther and said that Chinatown needs a social service agency."

Even though more than ten thousand residents called Chinatown home at that time and a Chinese Vietnamese community was growing in Uptown on the northside as thousands of Southeast Asian refugees settled in the city, there was not a single organization in the whole city that served these Chicagoans. Many new immigrants needed job counseling and English lessons. Without them, it was almost impossible to find meaningful work with humane hours and benefits.

Senior citizens needed help filling out state and federal government assistance forms to apply for services that were their rights as U.S. permanent residents, citizens, and residents of Chicago, yet are difficult to learn about or navigate when one doesn't read English.

These nine friends from Hong Kong started discussing plans to help Chinatown residents. When Grace Chiu suggested bringing on a younger woman from Hong Kong named Iris Ho who had come to Chicago to study at Loyola University, the number of founders became an even ten. Iris got to know the group when they went on bowling outings at the University of Illinois at Chicago. Since many of the founders already had full-time jobs or were still in graduate school, they could devote only a couple of hours on the weekends to their community work.

The Chicago Department of Human Services had a one-person office in Chinatown, so the ten friends wondered if this staff member might be able to offer more assistance to seniors and other Chinatown residents who had limited proficiency in English. The friends walked over to this storefront to speak in person to that one employee but found that he was able to offer only simple translation and interpretation services. This city worker had no capacity to help Chinatown residents fill out forms or teach ESL. The friends realized that this work could only get one if they did it on their own.

Eleanor had suggested starting an agency to provide services as needs came up, but it wasn't just a matter of renting out space at a driving school or finding an area to help seniors fill out forms. The friends needed to first gain the trust of the community before they could think on a larger scale. Trust was so important because it wasn't customary in Chinatown for people to discuss their problems or concerns with strangers, especially when it came to money and family issues. Traditionally, Chinese families relied on one another for help, and it was seen as a loss of face, or shameful, if someone asked a stranger for money or even non-monetary help. Chinatown residents were therefore accustomed to fending for themselves through family or benevolent associations, organizations formed in the nineteenth century in both the United States and Canada to help immigrants from southern China. It was unthinkable to ask the government or strangers at nonprofit organizations. The ten friends from Hong Kong learned about this trust issue the hard way.

| | |

The mid-to-late 1970s was an especially sensitive period because it was the tail end of the Cultural Revolution, a decade of massive upheaval throughout China. This upheaval often went unnoticed in other countries, particularly as news from

China did not flow freely even within the country, yet some leftist groups outside China idealized Mao Zedong for ending income disparity and social vices. So, earlier in the 1970s, when young community organizers set up a youth center in Chicago's Chinatown and tried to hand out pamphlets on the streets to advertise it, residents viewed them as Communist agitators. "There was some thought about indoctrination," C. W. Chan said. Most Chinatown residents had either fled China for Hong Kong after the 1949 Communist victory or had been in the United States before then and were wary of people with Communist sympathies.

This was especially noticeable in October each year around the time of the Double Ten parade as storefronts and public space in Chinatown flew the Chinese Nationalist flag, a red-and-blue flag with a twelve-pointed star that originated in China after the October 10, 1911 revolution to overthrow the Qing dynasty. This flag became the symbol of Taiwan after the Nationalist government fled to that island in 1949, while the new People's Republic of China (PRC) adopted a red flag with five golden stars. Nary a flag from the PRC would be seen in Chinatown in the 1970s or at any time before that. Given this anti-Communist sentiment, which was standard around the United States with the Cold War still in full force, these youth organizers didn't last very long in Chinatown.

The CASL founders arrived in Chinatown several years after the youth organizers and also tried to approach people on the streets to speak with them one-on-one to find out what kind of social services they could use. Although the majority of them had graduate-level social work backgrounds, they were perceived in the same light as the younger community organizers. And even though the CASL founders spoke Cantonese, longtime Chinatown residents still viewed them as outsiders because they mainly lived in Hyde Park or the suburbs. Their backgrounds as recent Hong Kong transplants also posed a problem for many Chinatown residents.

Hong Kong had had an element of leftist disruption a decade earlier that did make the news in Chinatowns around the world, so residents in Chicago's Chinatown had no way of knowing if the CASL founders also had ulterior motives. C. W. recalled, "Because this other group passed out flyers earlier in the 1970s, there was some suspicion in Chinatown about the CASL founders, even though our group of ten was in our early thirties and most were professionals with full-time jobs." The Chinatown old-timers felt it was best to keep their distance from these newcomers.

But the friends did not give up so quickly. They realized they would need to earn the trust of the community and prove they only wanted to help people, providing them with the tools to give themselves more meaningful lives. They knew it was certainly possible to gain trust in Chinatown, as Eleanor So, David Wong, and

Paul Ho had found after they started teaching ESL. They figured they would have more success in getting through to the community if they were to offer specific services like teaching English and filling out forms rather than approaching people on the street to ask how they could help.

| | |

In late 1976 and early 1977, Chicago ran a program to give senior citizens reduced rates on their utility bills, called the Circuit Breaker Tax Rebate program. From her work in East Chicago Heights, Bernie knew that offering senior citizens assistance in applying to an established program open to everyone in their age group would be a good way to engage with the Chinatown population. The Chinatown seniors wouldn't be singled out for a particular service but would simply join other Chicago seniors in applying for these utility bill reductions.

Bernie organized the friends to go to Chinatown to help seniors fill out forms and collate their Social Security records to apply for the Circuit Breaker Tax Rebate program. They were able to use space at the Chinese Consolidated Benevolent Association to set up tables and chairs in a welcoming environment. They also arrived with tea, coffee, and doughnuts. The seniors they encountered were receptive and appreciated the warm drinks and sweets.

The reception to this program was so positive that the following year, the ten friends decided to incorporate and form an official 501(c)(3) social service agency, which means CASL is officially recognized by the Internal Review Service as a charitable organization. Through a lawyer named Nicholas Stevenson, the friends met Peter Carey, another lawyer who volunteered pro bono legal advice to help them register as a nonprofit organization. Carey advised that they would need three U.S. citizens to form a 501(c)(3), yet of their group, only Anna Ho fit that qualification at the time.

This was a murky legal issue because the requirement could be interpreted as three current U.S. citizens or those with the intention of becoming U.S. citizens. If it were interpreted as the latter, that would be no problem for the ten founders. They were all at some point in the process of becoming U.S. citizens. Their educational and professional lives were in the Chicago area and none had plans to return to Hong Kong. But they feared if the person overseeing their application took the literal meaning of these terms—that is, that all three were required to already be U.S. citizens when they submitted their forms, their case would be rejected. Just to be sure, C. W. asked Raymond Lee, a mutual friend who introduced Bernie to Albert Wong, to be one of the signatories, along with Anna Ho and Peter Carey.

By February 1978, the Chinese American Service League (CASL, pronounced "castle") was official. Bernie came up with the name of the agency when she mentioned there was a Japanese American Service Committee already in Chicago. Theirs could go by a similar name. No one objected. And no one thought CASL would grow into the largest employer in Chinatown with an annual budget of $24 million forty-four years later. But back in 1978, they started on a much smaller scale.

Each founder chipped in $5 for a total of $50 to purchase stationery. They would also need a logo but didn't have money to hire a professional designer. Instead, Iris designed a logo of red straight-edged bubble letters that spelled "CASL." She left space in the middle of these bubble letters to write out the Chinese translation of Chinese American Service League. For that, Paul Ho wrote in yellow traditional Chinese characters, the writing style of Hong Kong, Taiwan, and other diaspora areas. Mainland China at that time was probably the only place to use simplified Chinese characters, which were devised in the 1950s to increase literacy in China. The English words for Chinese American Service League appeared in black writing beneath the logo. Almost half a century later, CASL still uses the same logo Iris and Paul created.

CASL was now official. As Eleanor recalled, "The founders all did this from their heart." They started to think about different programs that would be most beneficial to the community. For that, they would need to raise money and a lot of it.

3

Charitable Organizations and Connections

Before CASL was founded, Iris spent time at the local public library to research charitable organizations that grant funds to nonprofit organizations like CASL. In her research, she found information about United Way of Chicago. At the same time, Bernie spoke with Tak Mazuta, a colleague of hers in East Chicago Heights, who put her in touch with his neighbor Jerry Erickson at United Charities, the first charitable organization in Chicago going back to the 1850s. Now called Metropolitan Family Services, United Charities back in the late 1970s helped underserved families through a number of community centers in the city and suburbs.

Bernie was very impressed with Jerry's experience and his wealth of knowledge. She phoned to ask if he would be willing to meet with her and some of the other CASL founders to discuss their new agency. Jerry readily agreed and listened attentively, especially when they relayed their concerns about Chinatown teens. Gangs were a grave concern and a tempting way for teens to find belonging when they didn't have anywhere else to go after school but home. And if they dropped out of school, they were even more prone to joining a gang. Chinatown didn't have its own high school—and it still doesn't as of writing, although the Chicago Public Schools has allocated $50 million to build a new school just south of Chinatown—but it didn't even have after-school resources like a teen drop-in center or tutoring services in the late 1970s. When Jerry heard about these issues, he could see why an agency like CASL would be so vital to teens. "[Bernie] and I had a common concern about the needs of the people who were struggling to make it in difficult circumstances," Jerry recalled.

It would be difficult, if not impossible, for United Charities to run an organization in Chinatown because neither Jerry nor his staff spoke Chinese and the teens

Bernie wanted to help did not speak much English. Instead, Jerry came up with a plan for what he could offer Bernie and the other founders. He would donate space in his downtown Chicago office for a CASL staff member and a secretary, along with accounting services for a year to help the founders get off the ground. United Charities also helped Bernie and the founders to develop policies and procedural manuals, materials CASL would need to grow into a viable social service agency. Also through United Charities, Jerry used his connections to broker a deal whereby CASL could receive donations from the Chicago Community Trust and United Way of Chicago.

Some of the CASL founders met with Wiley Moore, vice president of United Way in Chicago. As they spoke to Moore about their concerns for Chinatown residents and the needs they had identified so far—senior socialization services, ESL, energy bill reduction assistance, and teen engagement—Bernie and the other founders not only gained an ally but listened attentively when Moore told them about some of the difficulties outsiders had had in Chinatown. They knew about the activists who had tried to start a youth center in the mid-1970s but now learned about an officer from Social Security who tried to help community members fill out forms, only to have doors slammed in his face. This Social Security officer did not speak Chinese, so to Chinatown residents, his purpose for knocking on their doors could have been anything. They probably did not expect someone to come to their homes to offer help. And when they saw him, they must have figured he was only there to check immigration status or some other kind of information that could easily incite fear. This information about the Social Security officer was very useful to Bernie and the other founders and was something they had also experienced when they had tried to talk to people in Chinatown one-on-one.

Moore appreciated CASL's aims in Chinatown and enthusiastically offered to help with their application to United Way. Because of this relationship, CASL received $16,000, and with Jerry Erickson's help they received another $16,000 from the Chicago Community Trust. Jerry would manage a total of $32,000 from these organizations. Grace Chiu credited Bernie with these successful grant applications because Bernie was the only one of the founders who had grant-writing experience in the United States thanks to her previous work in the Chicago suburbs. Now they would need to put together a board, mainly comprised of the founders, as well as hire an executive director.

To accomplish even a small portion of their goals, the founders knew that one of them would need to run CASL on a full-time basis and that would mean leaving a current job or graduate program. Eleanor recalled, "Our group of ten talked about funding and we all thought Bernie was the most qualified since she had already gotten funding for her first job in Chicago." Bernie agreed and took a gamble by quitting her job in East Chicago Heights to start up CASL as its executive director.

Bernie had the blessing of her mother, Virginia, who by then was spending six months at a time with her different children in Chicago, California, Wisconsin, Canada, and Hong Kong. Most of all, Bernie had the full support of her husband, Albert. When Bernie had worked for an employer, there was a defined start and finish to the workday. But now, heading up a new social service agency would involve long hours that would not end at the end of a traditional workday. Albert understood this and knew he would be the one to cook and take care of Jacinta and other domestic matters for their family each night.

In her new role, Bernie met with the board members mainly on the weekends when they had free time from their studies and jobs. Grateful to Jerry Erickson for his donation of free office space, Bernie spent her first two months working at CASL in downtown Chicago. But she knew it wasn't realistic that she'd use Jerry's office space forever. She did not want to outstay her welcome, and she also knew she could best help the community if she could work right in Chinatown. She could get to know Chinatown residents better if she could meet with them at an office that was within walking distance from their homes. In setting up a Chinatown office, CASL also found a lasting friend from a local banker who became a board member as well.

| | | |

Raymond Spaeth had been running the Lakeside Bank's Chinatown branch for more than a dozen years when Bernie walked into his office one blustery day in December 1979. Spaeth had developed a reputation as the main banker to give loans to Chinatown restaurants. Shortly before Bernie entered the bank, Spaeth's father had told him about the importance of giving back to the community where one works. At first, Spaeth felt he was giving back because he was providing a service to Chinatown restaurants that downtown Chicago banks wouldn't touch in the 1960s and 1970s, mainly because these other banks felt Chinatown was "foreign."

Spaeth's father saw things differently and advised his son to trust in the community in which he worked and to do more. One way of doing that was to not show favoritism and to not take advantage of unfair practices. Other banks south of Congress Parkway charged high interest rates because they knew they could. When there's a need and little supply, anything goes. But Spaeth didn't hike up his rates and instead offered fair loans to Chinatown businesses. His father also advised that he give back philanthropically. "Soon after this conversation," Spaeth

Bernie at her desk, donated by Ray Spaeth, at CASL's first permanent office on Cermak Road in 1979. Photo courtesy of the Chinese American Service League.

recalled, "Bernie walked into my bank and sat at my desk, asking for support for CASL."

Bernie found in Spaeth an eager listener. He advised her to manage CASL as if it were a business. Of course, CASL's mission would center on helping people, but he suggested she ensure there would be adequate funding for the programs CASL wanted to run. When Spaeth learned that Bernie had recently moved into a new office in Chinatown, he offered to donate a desk for her to use. Bernie was so touched by Spaeth's encouragement, advice, and the huge desk that she offered him a position on CASL's board of directors.

Shortly after she met Spaeth, Bernie returned to his bank when one of her case workers put her in charge of an inheritance. A worker at Won Kow Restaurant had recently passed away and it was discovered that he had left behind $80,000 in cash. While the deceased man's surviving relatives were being located, Bernie was put in charge of the cash and opened an account at Lakeside Bank for these relatives once they were found.

| | |

Early in the CASL years, Bernie asked Spaeth if he would be interested in joining a fishing daytrip CASL was organizing for kids. Phyliss Willett, another volunteer at CASL and wife of a bus company owner, also joined the outing. Willett, called "Gram Phyliss" by Bernie and the CASL staff, became a beloved volunteer and financial donor after reading about CASL in a 1984 *Chicago Tribune* article. She was an artist, costume designer, and the longtime widow of Howard L. Willett, the owner of a number of bus and truck companies. Gram Phyliss helped with art projects at CASL and brought her friends to fundraising events.

Spaeth was also game for the fishing trip, which turned out to include one hundred kids. "There were two ponds and enough kids to stand around every free spot in front of both ponds," Spaeth recalled decades later. "I bought bamboo poles with bobbers and every kid on the trip was able to take home a fish for dinner that day. They were either bluegills or sunfish." It was one of Spaeth's most memorable times with CASL. Spaeth started the $15,000 raffle at CASL's annual fundraisers, remained on the board for decades, and retired from Lakeside Bank in 2010. He went on to donate more than $100,000 to CASL until his death in 2022.

In the span of a year, give or take, Bernie and the other CASL founders had formed a board, were admitted into United Way of Chicago, and secured funding from other charitable foundations, the government, and corporations. With a budget in 1980 of almost $100,000 from these different organizations and a positive reception from Chinatown seniors—mainly due to the Circuit Breaker program—the founders were all set, apart from the need to win over the Chinatown leadership and the longtime alderman, or city council representative, of that district.

They would need more than coffee and doughnuts this time around.

4

The Dentist's Office

Dr. William K. K. Wan's dentistry is housed in a building with a shingled facade on the corner of Wentworth Avenue and Twenty-Third Street, three short blocks south of the Chinatown gate. Sandwiched between two souvenir shops, the entrance to Dr. Wan's office is inconspicuous with white lettering on the glass entrance door, showing in Chinese and English that Dr. Wan has earned both a DDS (doctor of dental surgery) and an MD (doctor of medicine) degree. He could have taken his skills anywhere in Chicago but chose to work in Chinatown. Dr. Wan has been a pillar of the community for decades.

In the mid-1970s, Dr. Wan's mother joined Eleanor So's English class and found great joy in spending time with her fellow classmates and her teacher. Dr. Wan would hear from his mother about these classes and was pleased she had found an activity she looked forward to on a regular basis. Mrs. Wan loved her new teacher so much that she came up with an idea that would give Eleanor more reason to stay in Chinatown. At this time, Eleanor had moved twenty miles west of Chicago to the suburb of Darien. Eleanor's husband was still working in Chicago, so he could drive her to Chinatown for her ESL classes. C. W. also drove Eleanor when she needed a ride. But those classes only occupied her mornings unless she took her students to the Museum of Science of Industry or another Chicago landmark. Dr. Wan's mother knew that her son could use a receptionist, so she suggested he hire Eleanor. With his mother as Eleanor's reference, Dr. Wan could not say no.

At this point, Eleanor, Bernie, and their friends had already filed paperwork to start CASL. Yet space was still an issue. Bernie was working in Jerry Erickson's downtown Chicago office but needed to look for something in Chinatown to provide a base from which the public could easily meet with her. Eleanor had an idea. "Dr. Wan's building had a couple stories and some space wasn't being used,"

Eleanor said. "So I asked if CASL could use it." She was specifically referring to an unoccupied second-floor storage room. The supplies stored there could easily be moved to another space in the building without blocking foot traffic. Eleanor envisioned a desk and a couple of chairs in that office for Bernie and anyone who needed to meet with her.

Eleanor asked Dr. Wan if Bernie could use the space for CASL's office until CASL found enough funding to rent a proper office in another building. Dr. Wan agreed to give the storage room to CASL free of charge, and Bernie soon moved in, ready to get to work. "The CASL founders would meet in my office at the beginning, usually on Saturdays," Dr. Wan recollected years later. "I was so impressed with their organization and by the way they wanted to serve the community."

The friendship between Eleanor, Dr. Wan, and his mother continued for decades after Eleanor moved to California in the early 1980s. "He invited me to his mother's birthday party every February," Eleanor said, "but it was hard to go in the winter. It was always a large banquet for all the seniors in the apartment building, and Dr. Wan offered to pay for my travel expenses, but the weather was prohibitive." Dr. Wan's mother lived past the age of one hundred.

The physical office space at Dr. Wan's dentistry, the seed grants, and the growing trust from Chinatown residents seemed as if they were great accomplishments so soon after CASL was founded just a year earlier, but Bernie and the founders knew they still needed something else to be truly successful in Chinatown. They needed to win over the alderman of their ward.

Chicago politics is defined by a mayor and the alderpeople that represent different wards or districts throughout the city. The mayor of Chicago may be blamed for problems in the city, but the alderpeople can have just as much clout—or sometimes more—than the mayor. In the late 1970s, Chinatown was in the 1st Ward, which was represented by Fred Roti, a longtime Chicago politician.

Roti was born in Chinatown, and his father ran a grocery store on Wentworth and Twenty-First Street. Legend had it that the senior Roti was a henchman for Al Capone, whose headquarters was close by on Michigan Avenue and Twenty-First Street and who supposedly accompanied his mother to church in Chinatown each Sunday.

Fred Roti had been an Illinois state senator in the 1950s until his district was rezoned and he moved over to Chicago city politics. After a stint as an inspector in the Department of Water and Sewers, he ran for alderman for the 1st Ward, a district that ran from Chinatown to City Hall, covering the Chicago Police

Department headquarters on State and Eleventh Streets as well as much of the financial and shopping district of the Loop. Roti quickly became part of "the machine" or the dominant Cook County Democratic Party that had a complete grip on Chicago's city hall and grew so influential that when Mayor Richard J. Daley died suddenly from a heart attack in 1976, Roti was one of several Chicago alderpeople who picked Michael Bilandic to succeed Daley.[1] In other words, Roti was not someone to deal with trivially.

As much as Bernie had accomplished in her previous job in East Chicago Heights, she was not keen on meeting Fred Roti. When CASL was founded in 1978, Chinatown was not on city hall's radar and it certainly was not the destination it is today. Anchored by the Chinatown gate on Wentworth and Cermak, the area was enclosed by Chicago Housing Authority high rises to the east, the Irish neighborhood of Bridgeport to the south, and abandoned railroad yards along the Chicago River to the north that were simmering in toxic waste. An additional boundary included the railway viaduct to the west. It was no wonder the residents of Chinatown stayed in their neighborhood. City hall did not see the value in developing Chinatown for business or more residential housing.

Back when CASL was starting out, Roti had a small Chinatown office with staff that neither spoke Chinese nor provided any assistance to residents apart from a free lunch program a few times a week. Roti may have thought that sufficed, but Bernie and the other CASL founders wanted to provide ESL classes, job counseling, senior citizen socialization, and youth programs. They needed Roti's blessing before they could expand their services. How they did that was a big question, as Roti did not have the most welcoming reputation.

Although Roti was born and raised in Chinatown, Chicago has never been known to be a melting pot and instead planned to keep communities isolated. Chinese immigrants first came to Chicago in the 1870s and settled around Van Buren and Clark Streets in what's now called the Loop. But this early Chinatown did not last long. In 1905, China boycotted America to protest anti-Chinese violence in the United States. In reaction to this boycott, Chicago landlords retaliated and raised the rents of their Chinese occupants to the extent that their homes became unaffordable. Half of the residents of this original Chinatown moved to the area around Cermak and Wentworth, a Croatian and Italian neighborhood. This area has been known as Chinatown since 1912. It was the neighborhood where Roti grew up.

Besides the prejudice against Chinese in Chicago, there was also the added fact that Bernie was an immigrant and a woman. No matter how well she spoke English, she feared Roti would not treat her as an equal. She felt the same sense of apprehension she had experienced her first year at Briar Cliff.

One day in Dr. Wan's office, Bernie mentioned these reservations about speaking with Roti. Dr. Wan had never seen Bernie shy away from anything and later recalled, "Alderman Roti thought that Bernie was a Communist and didn't want her in Chinatown. His district covered Chinatown and he had two people from city hall staff the office that was there to give out lunches. He didn't want that to go away. The city hall staff was only there two to three times a week and did nothing."

Bernie and her friends were not Chinatown insiders, so it would take some convincing to get Roti to agree to a new agency to help the very people his inadequate outreach office was not serving. "Roti had power when it came to zoning, businesses, and social services in Chinatown," Dr. Wan remembered. Since Dr. Wan was by then a trusted member of the Chinatown community, Bernie asked if he could go down to city hall to talk to Roti on her behalf.

City hall in 1979 was not a welcoming place. Mayor Richard J. Daley had died three years earlier, but the machine-style politics that defined his reign—reward your friends and punish your enemies—continued under Daley's successor, Michael Bilandic. When Dr. Wan entered Roti's office, he explained that Bernie and the other CASL founders simply wanted to serve the Chinatown community and were not the Communists or leftists he imagined. They had no political agenda that would interfere with gritty Chicago politicians. By the time Dr. Wan left Roti's office, he knew he could return to Bernie with Roti's blessing for CASL.

It would be the last time Bernie shied away from speaking with a politician.

| | |

Michael Bilandic's mayoral career would not last long. While Bernie was working out of the dentistry on Wentworth, she and millions of other Chicagoans and residents of northern Indiana experienced the worst blizzard in recorded history. A couple of inches of snow were predicted on a Saturday in mid-January 1979, but more than two feet covered the city in the matter of a weekend. Another foot would fall less than two weeks later. Completely unprepared for this avalanche of snow, Bilandic not only lost the confidence of his constituents, but he also lost the mayoral primary to Jane Byrne the following month.[2]

By the time Jane Byrne was on her way to becoming Chicago's first female mayor and the first woman to become mayor of a major American city, CASL had received funding from United Way and the Community Trust. CASL was never going to stay at Dr. Wan's second-floor storage room long term. Now that this funding came in, it was time to find a more permanent office space.

5

A Tale of Two Chinatowns

The CASL board started looking for a permanent home, but this didn't just entail finding available office to rent. It also meant convincing a potential landlord that CASL's work was worthwhile. That would not be so easy.

Many Chinatown residents still did not fully understand how CASL could help the community without an ulterior motive. Landlords felt especially wary about renting office space to Bernie and her staff. If CASL turned out to have a political agenda, the landlord who rented them space could also be implicated by association. By February 1979, just after the great blizzard, CASL found a captive audience in Peter Huey, the longtime owner of Won Kow Restaurant on Wentworth. Won Kow went on to become the oldest restaurant in Chinatown before it closed in 2018 after operating for ninety years.

Peter Huey arrived in Chicago in 1950 from Hong Kong and found work waiting tables at Won Kow. He gradually bought up real estate in Chinatown, eventually buying the Won Kow building with his brother, Robert.[1] One of Huey's buildings included 219 West Cermak, and in early 1979, it happened to have a vacant office on the second floor. The building was just down Cermak from the Chinatown arch.

Bernie's husband, Albert, knew Huey and asked him about this seven-hundred-square-foot space that included two offices and a small reception area that fit three chairs. Compared to the storage closet at Dr. Wan's dentistry, this space on Cermak seemed more than adequate for Bernie and her secretary, Man Ling. Huey was sympathetic to Albert's plea and could easily remember when he first arrived from Hong Kong almost thirty years earlier. He agreed to rent CASL this office space. Soon, the three chairs in the reception room were always filled.

With that hurdle out of the way, Bernie and the CASL board faced another obstacle: getting the blessing of the Chinatown residents. Securing Alderman Roti's approval was difficult enough, but Chinatown in the late 1970s was overseen by two different groups, one mainly Anglophone and the other Sinophone. To be able to serve all residents of Chinatown, Bernie and C. W., president of the CASL board, knew they had to obtain endorsements from the leaders of these two groups.

Bernie went first to see a man named Ping Tom since he, too, was seen as a Chinatown outsider in many ways.

| | |

Ping Tom was the leader of the English-speaking faction of Chinatown and a founder of the Chinatown Chamber of Commerce. Born and raised in Chicago, he attended John C. Haines Elementary School in Chinatown before winning a scholarship to the Francis W. Parker School, an elite private school on the northside that spanned kindergarten to high school. It was at Parker that he developed an appreciation for different cultures and a strong sense of confidence. Tom went on to earn a six-year joint bachelor's–juris doctor degree at Northwestern University. And although he appreciated his educational opportunities outside of Chinatown, his heart remained in the community where he grew up.

As an adult, Tom became the president of a number of different family businesses in Chinatown, some started by his father Tom Y. Chan, a fundraiser for Chinese Nationalist leaders Sun Yat-sen and Chiang Kai-shek,[2] the latter of whom took the Nationalist Party to Taiwan in 1949 after the Communist Party won the civil war in China. Because of this long history of supporting the Nationalists, Chicago's Chinatown residents in the 1970s mainly backed the government of the Republic of China on Taiwan.

Before Chinatown was developed into the thriving community it is today, Tom helped negotiate with city and state officials to clean up the thirty acres of contaminated wasteland along the Chicago River adjacent to Chinatown. This space had been used for decades as Santa Fe railroad yards but had long been abandoned and left to fall into decay. Tom was on the boards of several downtown Chicago banks and had clout in city hall. He easily moved between the Loop and Chinatown, comfortable and respected in both spheres, and in later years advised Mayors Harold Washington and Richard M. Daley.

Bernie met with Tom and explained CASL's desire to help people in Chinatown, especially new immigrants and the elderly. Because of his own interest in improving the lives of Chinatown residents, he saw great value in CASL's mission and gave Bernie his blessing. And as the English secretary of the Chinatown Consolidated

Benevolent Association (CCBA), Tom was in a position to introduce Bernie and the other founders to the other Chinatown leader, Wayne Sit, president of the CCBA.

Chinatowns around the United States all had a CCBA. Initially, they existed mainly to send the remains of deceased Chinese Americans back to their ancestral homes in China, but as the needs of these communities grew, the roles of CCBAs expanded to include meal programs, ESL classes for seniors, and Chinese classes for children, to name a few. Family associations in Chicago's Chinatown worked with CCBA as did the Chinese Freemasons. These groups all tended to side with the Republic of China on the issue of Taiwan, but the CASL founders wanted their agency to remain neutral—favoring neither Taiwan nor the PRC—so they planned to work independently from CCBA, the family associations, and the Chinese Freemasons.

Bernie would be joined by C. W. when she made her next visit, this time to Wayne Sit.

| | |

Unlike Ping Tom, Wayne Sit spoke Chinese. Sit was born in Toisan, a county in Guangdong Province that received the most remittances among any place in China during the Gold Rush and building of the U.S. railroads in the middle of the 1800s. The movie star Anna May Wong's family origins were from Toisan, as were those of author Maxine Hong Kingston. The Toisan dialect is different from Cantonese and for decades was the dominant language in Chicago's Chinatown, going back to the earliest Chinese immigrants who arrived in the mid-1800s. The dominant language in Chicago's Chinatown started changing in the 1970s and '80s as more Cantonese-speaking immigrants from Hong Kong—like Bernie and the other CASL founders—arrived in the city. Now Mandarin is the predominant language spoken in Chinatown after immigration from mainland China increased starting in the 1990s.

Sit's father received his U.S. naturalization after sailing to Canada and crossing the country by train until he came to Rouse's Point, New York, on the Canada–United States border. The elder Sit was detained by U.S. border guards for violating the Chinese Exclusion Act of 1882 and was taken to jail. At his court hearing, a caring stranger in the courtroom claimed that Sit was his nephew and therefore had a right to citizenship. This loophole in the xenophobic prohibition of Chinese immigrants was possible thanks to the 1906 San Francisco earthquake. A fire erupted after the earthquake, and the government office that held birth records was burned to the ground. Chinese Americans could claim relatives or neighbors back in China were their sons or daughters and there was no way to prove otherwise because the birth certificate office with the largest Chinese population in the United States no longer had records.

The judge had no way to confirm Sit's relationship to this stranger, so he adjudicated in Sit's favor and granted him naturalized citizenship. Now free, Sit could frequently travel back and forth between the United States and China and went on to sponsor many family members to immigrate to the States. His son Wayne, back in China, was granted U.S. citizenship at birth because by the time he was born, his father was already a U.S. citizen. Wayne Sit's father had also donated funds to Sun Yat-sen.

Educated at the Pui Ying boarding school in Canton (now Guangzhou), Wayne Sit married in China. At the age of twenty, he moved to Hughes, Arkansas, to help run a family grocery store. This was his father's idea. He wanted his son to experience how hard he had had to work in the United States to support their family. The elder Sit hoped some of his hard work would rub off on his son, but Arkansas would prove to be just a stepping-stone.

Sit's brother-in-law ran upscale Chinese restaurants in downtown Chicago that catered to non-Chinese diners with chop suey and chow mein as well as dishes like pork tenderloin and chicken à la king. These restaurants served a clientele about as socioeconomically distant from Chinatown as possible. Sit was called to Chicago to help run one of these eateries.

Soon, he opened his own restaurant, South Pacific, at 30 West Randolph, that captured the Polynesian craze of the time.[3] He hired women to dance hula in grass skirts and men to perform fire dances dressed in only in loincloths. Business was lucrative and Sit felt financially secure, but something was missing. Although he, his wife, and children lived outside of Chinatown on the northside, Sit felt connected to the Toisan community in Chinatown and wanted to give back to residents there. He went on to run the CCBA.

Sit had a good first impression of CASL when he learned that Esther Wong's father had also graduated from Pui Ying in Canton and that C. W. had graduated from Pui Ying in Hong Kong. But there was another reason Sit agreed to endorse CASL. He was one of the few in Chinatown who recognized the problems that held back residents. Sit's daughter, Elaine, recalled a time before her father met with Bernie and C. W.: "He once spoke to a reporter at the *Chicago Sun-Times* and mentioned that Chinatown had problems. There were at-risk youth, low-income seniors, and low-income immigrants in need, and that social services could really help them. The problem was that it wasn't customary in Chinese communities to ask for help from outsiders. It was seen as a loss of face and something families took care of. But if people didn't have family in Chicago or if their family was low income, it was hard to get by." Yet instead of feeling relieved that Sit had exposed these problems all in the name of trying to find a solution, Chinatown residents were embarrassed.

But Sit wouldn't stop at that. He lobbied Chicago's city hall to fund a three-course lunch for low-income seniors who were able to get to CCBA, although that left out seniors who couldn't leave home and low-income immigrants and teens. Elaine Sit also said that her father "was willing to acknowledge the issues that CCBA could not address in their capacity." The social workers from Hong Kong suddenly seemed appealing.

Yet Bernie, C. W., and Sit knew that not everyone at CCBA would warm to CASL. Sit had already revealed the issues that plagued the area. Now a group was willing to help, even though they were from Hong Kong and did not all speak the Toisan dialect. The CASL founders and Chinatown residents also differed in their educational levels. Many of the founders had studied at one of the two elite universities in Hong Kong and at the University of Chicago, all of which may as well have been on a different planet to many recent immigrants. But when Sit told his CCBA colleagues that the CASL founders were to be trusted, many took him at his word because he was held in such high regard.

In an initial meeting with the CCBA and the Chinese American Civic Council, Bernie and C. W. met in front of a panel from both groups. They were asked to declare their positions on the Panama Canal. Although it seemed completely unrelated to Chicago and Chinatown, C.W. knew it was the panel's way of figuring out Bernie and C.W.'s politics.

"If we thought the canal should be given back to Panama, we would be seen as Communists, whereas if we thought the U.S. should hold on to it, we would be seen as patriots," C. W. recalled. Instead, C. W. simply answered that he and Bernie were there to talk about Chinatown. "We had productive conversations with the panel, and they realized CASL had great intentions."

With the green light from both Ping Tom and Wayne Sit, as well as the endorsement of Alderman Roti, CASL could now operate as it wished.

||||||||||||||||||||||||||||||||||||||||||||||||||||||||||||||||||||||||||||||||||||||||||||||||||||||||||||||||||||||

Ping Tom Memorial Park

Ping Tom was an early champion of CASL and without his support, the league never would have succeeded.

When Chinatown lost Hardin Park in 1962 due to the construction of the Dan Ryan Expressway, the city vowed to put in another park but was slow to deliver on their promise. Several decades later, Tom started to campaign for a new park in the abandoned railway yards along the Chicago River. Shortly after his death in 1995, the Chicago Park District finally started to develop one. It has since become one of the most beloved parks in the city and is rightfully called Ping Tom Memorial Park. It's just a quick walk from CASL's current location, which also occupies part of the same land that used to be part of the abandoned railway yard.

Like many attractions in Chinatown, Ping Tom Park has another CASL connection. In the mid-1990s, a young landscape architect named Ernie Wong returned to his hometown of Chicago to help his architect father work on an elementary school in Chinatown. Ernie Wong knew Chinatown from his youth as a place to eat but had never envisioned working there. Yet when he heard of the development of Ping Tom Park, he inquired and ended up winning the project. His firm, site design group, has since become one of the leading landscape design groups in the United States. Bernie recruited Ernie to become a member of the CASL board, and as of this writing, he's the board member with the longest seniority.

Thanks to Ernie's vision, Ping Tom Park stands out because of its elegant Chinese features. Along a path, painted red fencing with Chinese motifs match the metalwork of the park's pavilion, styled after a Chinese pagoda. Next to the pagoda is a bronze bust of Ping Tom wearing his signature large, framed glasses. His name is engraved in both English and Chinese over the years he lived, 1935–1995. These features, along with native plants and rolling prairies, make Ping Tom Park one of the most scenic in Chicago.

Ernie is also the chair of the summer dragon boat races—held along Ping Tom Park's riverfront—that attract racers and viewers from around the Midwest. The Chicago Water Taxi runs a regular route during the warmer months to take passengers to and from Ping Tom Park and Union and Ogilvy Stations in the Loop.

Over the years, the park has expanded to include a boathouse where people can rent kayaks and a field house featuring a swimming pool, gymnasium, meeting rooms, fitness center, and skyline patio. The field house is named after Leonard M. Louie, another long-standing CASL board member and the uncle of former CASL board president Jim Mark.

There is now a Ping Tom Advisory Council that commissions cultural and bilingual programming in the park that anyone can enjoy, no matter their background. The advisory council is also responsible for commissioning colorful murals under the Eighteenth Street bridge that incorporate elements from Chinese culture, advising on repairs to structures in the park, and organizing regular cleanups.

PART II

The Busy 1980s

6

In the Spirit of the Settlement Movement

The settlement house movement started in Chicago in the late 1880s to help poor immigrants rise above their conditions. Settlement houses provided services like job training, meal programs, and English lessons but also fought the stigma that people were poor by choice. The first settlement house was the famous Hull-House, founded by Jane Addams and Ellen Gates Starr,[1] social reformers who rented the second floor of a house built for Charles J. Hull, an early settler in Chicago.[2] Hull-House was located in a poor immigrant community on the Near West Side, two miles northwest from the neighborhood that would become Chinatown in 1912. In the late 1800s, the Near West Side was plagued by open sewage and uncollected garbage as well as substandard housing and job opportunities that could barely keep families afloat.

Addams and Starr both came from wealth and believed that educated volunteers like themselves should live among the people they aimed to help. Rather than thinking people were poor out of laziness, alcoholism, or a lack of religion, settlement house organizers viewed poverty as a result of limited opportunities. They recognized that this was especially true when it came to education and employment, where just by luck some people never had to work hard to get into a school with many resources, while others couldn't afford to give up a measly wage to look for decent educational opportunities.

Social workers helped people in impoverished communities develop skills and confidence to find better jobs and education, either of which could help people bring themselves out of poverty. Addams and Starr felt they had the most success when they understood the communities they were trying to help, but this couldn't happen if social workers returned home to comfortable living conditions at the end of each day. There would be no way they could truly comprehend what it meant to be poor. The residence model that Addams and Starr promoted would become popular among the early settlement houses such as Hull-House. By 1911, there were thirty-five settlement houses in Chicago.

Settlement houses were not typically part of Chinatowns across the United States because family associations and churches served many of the same purposes. Churches were acceptable thanks in part to missionaries in China and Hong Kong who had established schools in poor areas there.

In his book about San Francisco's Chinatown, *Building Community, Chinatown Style*, Gordon Chin writes about the community development movement, a more recent model that picked up traction in the 1960s. Chinatowns around the country experienced poverty, yet Chinese churches and benevolent associations could not always solve all these issues on their own, especially when it came to affordable housing. The community development movement, unlike the settlement house movement, did not focus on immigrant communities, but it was inevitable that the people they helped included new immigrants. The community development movement began in different boroughs of New York City as well as inner cities and rural areas around the country.

Chin became a leader of San Francisco's Chinatown Community Development Center decades ago and recognized that the term "community development" usually referred to housing. But he also found it a useful term to describe his community in a way that went beyond where one lives "because it encompasses other roles we play and other interests besides affordable housing, such as parks and playgrounds, social services, and transportation to name a few."[3]

Since many of the CASL founders came from social work backgrounds, they were familiar with the settlement house and community development movements. CASL was never meant to be a residential center, but Bernie believed in the idea of living among the people she wanted to help. So around the time CASL was incorporated as a nonprofit organization, she, her husband, Albert, and their daughter, Jacinta, moved eight miles north from their home in Chicago's South Shore neighborhood to Chinatown. This way, Bernie could gain a better sense of what the community needed. Her move also showed the residents that she was deeply invested in Chinatown.

The CASL founders recognized the need for new services as more Chinese immigrants and refugees arrived in Chicago, both in the northside neighborhood of Uptown and in the southside's Chinatown. These areas were a natural destination for these new immigrants for a number of reasons. Journalist Lev Golinkin has written about the importance of community when it comes to immigration and fitting in: "Cities have dense concentrations of low-level, immigrant-ready jobs coupled with public transportation, Laundromats, pharmacies, grocery stores, and other conveniences of Western life squeezed into a few blocks. What's most crucial is that all those jobs and institutions are staffed by and cater to [native language] speakers, which eliminated the crippling effect of the language barrier. The whole idea was to ease the lonely transition to America by plugging isolated refugees into long-established linguistic, ethnic, and immigrant networks."[4]

As Eleanor So had experienced with her ESL students, there had to be a fine balance between feeling comfortable in a place like Chinatown that had the linguistic, ethnic, and immigrant networks Golinkin writes about, while at the same time learning the skills and confidence to go beyond the boundaries of this enclave to become comfortable in the whole of Chicago and all it has to offer.

To find this balance, after launching the Circuit Breaker program, the CASL founders wanted to help senior citizens overcome the isolation and depression many suffered from having never left the confines of Chinatown. Seniors are often the most overlooked age group in this country, and immigrants who come to the United States as retirees often experience a type of culture shock their grown children can't always understand. Grown children either work or study outside the home and can more easily make friends or simply talk to other adults on a daily basis. But for seniors who mainly stay at home and do not speak English, it's difficult to socialize and find a welcoming community.

CASL sought out funding from the Chicago Department of Aging & Disability to start counseling services as well as a program to help seniors socialize in their community and find purpose in their twilight years. Eleanor had taken her class of seniors to the Museum of Science and Industry and to the Playboy Club, but it wasn't always practical for CASL staff and a growing number of volunteers to take seniors on outings using Chicago's public transportation. As would become one of its trademarks, CASL looked at its own resources and was fortunate that its first part-time employee, C. P. Louie, offered his van to drive seniors around Chicago and the suburbs so they could see what lay beyond Chinatown. For some of these seniors, it was their first time seeing a forest in the United States. The smiles on their faces and their exclamations of wonder proved to the CASL staff and volunteers that these services were certainly well worth the effort. CASL started a resocialization program at this time, which has become one of its most popular services and remains strong today.

| | |

But not all issues had an easy solution. In 1978, when the Hong Kong friends came together to form CASL, Chicago was just starting to witness a new influx of refugees. After the fall of Saigon in 1975, U.S. troops left in defeat as South

Vietnam and North Vietnam were unified into one country, the Socialist Republic of Vietnam. For centuries, Vietnam as a whole had been home to a large ethnic Chinese population, mainly in the southern part of the country. If Chinese Vietnamese could speak a Chinese dialect, for the most part it would be Cantonese. In 1978, Vietnam invaded Kampuchea, now Cambodia, ending almost half a decade of Khmer Rouge terror and genocide in that country. China was aligned with Kampuchea and the murderous Khmer Rouge regime, so in early 1979, Chinese troops attacked Vietnam on the China-Vietnam border in retaliation of Vietnam's invasion of Kampuchea.

The fighting didn't last a month, but the repercussions from this conflict would cause great damage to Vietnam's ethnic Chinese population, as they became scapegoats for the problems in Vietnam. No longer seen as fellow countrymen, they started to leave Vietnam in the late 1970s by any means possible. These escapes often meant dangerous sea voyages on makeshift boats or rafts. It was not unusual for refugees to die at sea.

The CASL founders were in the position to know about the influx of ethnic Chinese refugees for a couple of important reasons. First, although the founders had left Hong Kong years before 1978, most still had family there and would have learned that Hong Kong was quickly becoming a safe haven for Vietnamese refugees by the end of that year and early 1979. Second, Chicago had agreed to take in thousands of Vietnamese refugees at this time, many of them ethnic Chinese.

CASL suddenly had a crisis on its hands.

Since Bernie and her staff were on the southside, it was difficult to adequately help new refugees who settled in Uptown on the northside. There was already a growing Vietnamese community in Uptown from the first wave of refugees in 1975, so it made sense for these new arrivals to settle there. Uptown also had a thriving Chinese community, which had mostly moved there in the 1970s from the last of the original Chinatown on Van Buren Street in the Loop. An entrepreneur named Jimmy Wong purchased inexpensive property on both sides of Argyle Street and provided financial help for small business owners, but the area never took off as a "New Chinatown." Instead, Uptown has become more known for the Vietnamese refugees who settled there, including ethnic Chinese.

Many suburban church groups helped settle refugees, but it wasn't so easy for some people to live isolated in the suburbs without an easy way to get around. The city with its conveniences—namely, Asian grocery stories, more jobs, and public transportation—often seemed more appealing than the suburban sprawl.

Language was also a major deciding factor. Although not all ethnic Chinese refugees spoke Cantonese, they did speak Vietnamese and could get along best in a neighborhood where others spoke the same language.

| | |

Bernie and the CASL board didn't set out to become involved with refugee resettlement until Ed Silverman contacted them for help. Silverman was the founder and leader of the Illinois Bureau of Refugee and Immigrant Services and came into this role after then—Illinois governor Dan Walker hired him to help with the influx of Vietnamese refugees after the fall of Saigon in 1975. Silverman and Walker both thought this program would be a temporary one and didn't imagine Vietnamese refugees would continue to seek new homes for the next two decades. The Illinois Bureau of Refugee and Immigrant Services ended up becoming an established department in the Illinois state government. Silverman also helped write the 1980 Refugee Act, which was signed by President Jimmy Carter and would allow for an additional ten million refugees to be settled in the United States.[5]

In 1979, Silverman asked CASL if it could help resettle these new Vietnamese refugees because so many were ethnic Chinese and CASL was the only social service agency in Chicago working with the Chinese community. CASL still works very closely with the Illinois Bureau of Refugee and Immigrant Services and is one of three dozen social service agencies under the umbrella of the Illinois Welcoming Center, the bureau's initiative to provide culturally appropriate services to refugees and immigrants in Illinois.

CASL hired a young refugee counselor named Shing Lee to work in Uptown and to report back to Bernie and the CASL board about the needs of this growing community, mostly related to housing and job counseling. Lee was especially helpful with Vietnamese refugees because he could converse with them in two of the dialects the refugees spoke: Cantonese and Teochownese. Many immigrants from Teochow, or Chaozhou in southern China, settled in Hong Kong and around Southeast Asia, including Vietnam. Even if ethnic Chinese refugees from Vietnam also spoke Cantonese, they sometimes preferred to converse in Teochownese if that was their mother tongue.

Also in the late 1970s, Bernie learned about a social work graduate student at the University of Illinois at Chicago (UIC). Mike Chan was also from Hong Kong and had attended college in Taiwan where he had become fluent in Mandarin, the official language spoken there and in mainland China.

As would become her custom, Bernie would learn about someone who could be of value to CASL and would try to bring him or her on as either an employee, board member, or volunteer. Gone were the days of Bernie's isolated nights in her college library. As Chan remembered, "I learned from Bernie that it was hard to say no and that she would never quit and would always give 110 percent. She was

Shing Lee, far right, making a home visit to check in on newly settled refugees from Vietnam in 1980. Lee would staff CASL's Uptown office for a short time during the influx of ethnic Chinese refugees from Vietnam. Photo courtesy of the Chinese American Service League.

so positive and had such a great spirit. Her leadership galvanized people, and she was always very respectful and had amazing energy."

Linda Yu had the same feelings about Bernie's dedication to CASL and also had a hard time saying no. Not everyone would appreciate her style, but it was Bernie's commitment to Chinatown that resulted in a core group of staff and management that stayed at CASL for decades.

"Bernie recruited me to volunteer at CASL when I was a student," Chan recalled. He was studying for his master of social work degree and she was desperate for help with Vietnamese refugees.

It wasn't unusual for someone to work or volunteer at CASL for a number of months or years, only to return to work there. Chan volunteered at CASL from 1978 to 1980 and was such a cherished member of the agency that Bernie hired him full time in 1981 after he graduated from UIC. In working with Vietnamese refugees, Chan found that many suffered from post-traumatic stress disorder, which came from living in war zones and trying to survive daily bombings only to leave everything behind to start over in the United States, not to mention weeks at sea with no guarantee of survival.

"No one expected there to be that many refugees from Vietnam at that time," Chan recounted decades later. "The refugees spoke Vietnamese. Some spoke

Cantonese and Mandarin. Many of the refugees had lost their Chinese-language skills because their families had been in Vietnam for so long and had assimilated." Chan's Cantonese and Mandarin abilities came in handy for the refugees who could speak more Chinese than English.

"Most of the refugees were businesspeople in Vietnam, so had no experience with manual labor and had to learn sills to get jobs in Chicago," Chan said. "The refugees were well-off in Vietnam but lost everything and had to start over in the U.S. They were bosses back in Vietnam."

Learning manual labor skills in the United States was also a daunting prospect for someone who didn't know the language, was unfamiliar with the culture and climate, and was suddenly responsible for paying bills without a steady income. Chan was able to connect some of the refugees with the Washburne Culinary and Hospitality Institute on Chicago's southside, where they could learn marketable skills. He also made connections in the local manufacturing industry—namely, clothing and machinery—and introduced employers to refugees who had run their own factories back in Vietnam.

Some of his lasting connections involved the Ambassador East Hotel in Chicago's ritzy Gold Coast district, where Chan convinced the housekeeping manager to employ Vietnamese refugees, most of whom were women. "Before I moved to New York," Chan said, "I ran into some women I had placed in jobs at the Ambassador East and they were so grateful to me. They'd worked there for twenty to thirty years." While he was at CASL in the 1980s, Chan also provided counseling to help refugees with job retention, working with them on issues that may cause them to otherwise become absent from work.

| | |

During the influx of ethnic Chinese from Vietnam, Duc Huang and his family settled in Chicago after fleeing Vietnam in 1978. The Huangs also saw a need for services when it came to helping Chinese speakers of dialects spanning from Cantonese, Fukienese, Hakka, and Teochownese with resettlement and preserving their culture. While many of these refugees had spoken Vietnamese outside their homes before they left Vietnam and even after they settled in Chicago, Huang worried they would lose their Chinese identity if they couldn't have an opportunity to engage in activities centered on Chinese culture and language.

Most Chicagoans did not differentiate between the Vietnamese refugees who mainly arrived around the fall of Saigon in 1975 and the ethnic Chinese who settled in Chicago in the late 1970s. There were already social service agencies in Uptown that served Southeast Asian clients from Vietnam, Cambodia, and Laos, but none of these agencies specifically tailored their programs to ethnic Chinese.

Huang's daughter Yman Vien recalled, "My father felt very strongly that there be language- and culturally appropriate services for ethnic Chinese refugees. He was instrumental in changing the language and perception for the new influx of refugees from Vietnam in the late 1970s to make sure people knew they were Chinese and that they suffered because of their ethnicity back in Vietnam."

Soon after settling in Chicago, Duc Huang started teaching Chinese to ethnic Chinese who came from assimilated families in Southeast Asia. He also organized activities around the Mid-Autumn Festival, or Moon Festival. Around that time, Vien worked in social services when Jewish Vocational Services hired her to assist with their Chinese- and Vietnamese-speaking clients.

In 1980, Huang and Vien founded a social service agency to specifically help ethnic Chinese from Vietnam, Laos, and Cambodia. A year later, they would receive funding and incorporate as the Chinese Mutual Aid Association (CMAA). Bernie and Vien would work closely together for years to come, both serving on immigrant and refugee coalitions. "Bernie showed me that a woman could lead an organization and fundraise nonstop," Vien recalled. "She also showed me that leading a nonprofit organization like CMAA or CASL was a noble profession and something to be very proud of."

Besides the friendship between the two leaders of these agencies, a number of CASL staff would go on to become executive directors at CMAA.

| | | |

CASL could hardly keep up with the need for services. Its first initiative for seniors, the Circuit Breaker Tax Rebate program, had become so popular that the agency started a program to help elderly residents in Chinatown sign up for Social Security. Many seniors qualified for Social Security but just didn't know how to apply or even that it was part of their rights as permanent residents or U.S. citizens.

When CASL started Social Security registration, word spread and lines formed down the stairs and out the door onto Cermak. The Social Security Administration took notice and sent their own team to CASL on a monthly basis to help Bernie and her staff keep up with the demand. CASL even had a staff member, Vera Wong, who worked with seniors and went on to take a job with the city of Chicago's Department on Aging.

In the first part of the 1980s, CASL developed a close relationship with another part of the federal government, the U.S. Immigration and Naturalization Service (INS) office in Chicago, which was part of the U.S. Department of Justice. A. D. Moyer was the INS district director in Chicago and, just as with the Social Security Administration, sent some of his officers to help train CASL's staff on immigration regulations and procedures. Moyer also provided this training to the CASL board so they would understand the inner workings of the INS. With more knowledge about the process, CASL staff could help Chinatown residents fill out the needed immigration paperwork. The relationship between CASL and the INS became so close that Moyer offered social worker Mike Chan a job at the Chicago INS office in 1984. Chan went on to oversee naturalization and was even sent to Guangzhou to clean up the backlog of cases at the INS's office there. Chan later moved to New York where he now serves as a minister.

Although Bernie was sad to lose Chan from CASL, she understood that his services could also be served well at the INS. This was a hallmark of Bernie's mentorship. Employees worked hard under her wing at CASL, but if they went into other jobs, they were always very well trained with excellent management skills. Thanks to A. D. Moyer and Mike Chan, CASL enjoyed a close relationship with the INS and could successfully assist clients with their immigration applications, a process that could otherwise be daunting as Bernie had learned when she was trying to help Herman So's father and sister, Hanna, get to the United States just a few years earlier.

| | |

As Eleanor So experienced when she taught ESL, many Chinatown residents were not accustomed to making regular appointments to see a doctor. The language barrier was a problem, but there was also an issue with time. People who worked long hours, sometimes six or seven days a week, had little flexibility to see a doctor during normal office hours. So in 1980, CASL tried to make access to health checkups easier for Chinatown residents and initiated screenings through Chicago's Department of Health and Blue Cross Blue Shield. These screenings were free of charge to Chinatown residents and were mainly geared toward seniors, the segment of the population that overall had the most difficulty leaving home to see a doctor because of mobility and language barriers.

At these health fairs, large vans and trucks that looked like recreational vehicles parked on Cermak just in front of CASL's office. Bernie, her staff, and volunteers set out tables on the sidewalk that would make it easy for seniors and other Chinatown residents to fill out screening forms and receive a basic physical with a health-care professional in the privacy of the vans. They would discuss blood pressure, cholesterol, heart disease, and diabetes, some of the most pressing health concerns in elderly populations. These screenings also touched on the health risks of smoking. Cigarette advertising had just been banned from television and radio nine years earlier and the U.S. surgeon general had only released the government-issued report on the risks of smoking in 1964, although Illinois would not ban smoking in public buildings, restaurants, and bars until 2008. So during CASL's

CASL's first health screening, on the sidewalk of Cermak Road just under their second-floor office. Photo courtesy of the Chinese American Service League.

early health screenings, the risks of cigarette smoking fell in between the first reports on the ill effects of smoking and an all-out indoor ban.

There was no way CASL could have held a health fair on this scale inside their small office. There was also little chance that seniors walking down Cermak would have ever learned about the fair if it hadn't been held outside. These efforts not only helped the community by providing much-needed services but also brought more visibility to CASL. Anyone strolling along that stretch of Cermak could not help but notice CASL's presence and growing acceptance.

By this time, Bernie and the CASL board—under C. W.'s leadership and Esther's continuing dedication—had secured government and other corporate grants from Continental Bank, Harris Bank, and R. R. Donnelley & Sons. Thus, CASL started the 1980s with an operating budget of almost $100,000. As of this writing, CASL's budget in 2022 was $24 million.

And what began as an office of one had turned into an organization of twelve staff members and sixty volunteers. Like the settlement house philosophy of relying on volunteers, CASL was able to benefit from people in the community who wanted to give back. In 1980 alone, CASL helped more than 1,100 people, including placing 222 adults in jobs or training programs.

The key to CASL's success was getting out the word that its staff and volunteers were there to serve the community. Coincidentally, a young Chinese American reporter had just arrived from San Francisco and would help amplify CASL's message to Chicagoans outside Chinatown, raising millions of dollars along the way.

7

Linda Yu to the Rescue

In early 1979, a young broadcast journalist took a job with Chicago's NBC Channel 5. Linda Yu was the first Chinese American reporter on the air in Chicago and had previously reported from Los Angeles, Portland, Oregon, and mostly recently, San Francisco's ABC Channel 7. Her arrival in Chicago did not escape Bernie's eyes.

A year into what would turn out to be Linda's illustrious thirty-seven-year career in Chicago, Bernie was struggling to bring young Herman So's father and sister from China before his mother passed away from cancer. Politicians had the power to make deals behinds the scenes, but the early 1980s was a difficult time because the United States and China had restored relations only the year before. Bernie knew that more publicity for the So family's case would only help their chances of reunification.

That's when Linda received a call from Bernie out of the blue. Listening to Bernie's account of the So family's story, Linda felt an affinity with Herman, Hanna, and their parents. Linda's own family had left China for Hong Kong when she was a young child. China's civil war in the mid-1940s caused upheaval across the country and Linda's family felt they would be safer in British Hong Kong. Linda's father was studying at a seminary in Philadelphia at the time and planned to return to his family in Hong Kong upon his graduation. But by late 1949, the Communists had won the war in China and Linda's father deemed it best to stay in the United States and for his family join him there. Linda felt the So family's story was hers, too. "We had nothing when we came," Linda recalled. If people hadn't helped them when they arrived, she said, she and her family wouldn't have gotten as far as they had in the United States. "I felt I must help."

Linda aired a news segment about the rush to bring Mr. So and Hanna to Chicago before Mrs. So passed away. With this television story and all of the

Chinatown residents waiting to meet with Bernie at her Cermak Road office. Photo
courtesy of Jacinta Wong.

politicians Bernie reached out to for help, the proper paperwork was processed
in the United States and Mr. So and Hanna were able to get to Chicago to say
goodbye. After that, Bernie called on Linda whenever she needed help or thought
publicity could help a cause CASL was fighting for. "After that, when there was
any need, she would call me," Linda said. "You can't say no to Bernie."

| | | |

Not long after CASL moved into the Cermak office, it became apparent that
space was again an issue. As Linda noticed when she arrived to report her story,
a tiny office reached by a steep set of stairs was hardly the ideal space for a social
service agency. For one, few people could fit into Bernie's office. Second, it wasn't
safe for senior citizens to walk up such a steep staircase, let alone to wait for an
extended amount of time on the stairs. The CASL office went on to expand by
renting the adjacent office space when it became available, but even that was too
small for the number of people seeking help.

By 1983, a number of the original founders had already moved away from
Chicago. Grace Chiu and her husband left first, followed by Iris Ho, Anna and
Paul Ho, and Eleanor So. They kept in touch and abreast of the changes at CASL

Bernie with broadcast journalist Linda Yu soon after they first met. Photo courtesy of Jacinta Wong.

from those who stayed behind: Bernie, Esther and David Wong, and Heidi and C. W. Chan. CASL employed seventeen staff members in 1983 to help with existing programs as well as the new ones it had in mind for the near future. Yet the long lines of people waiting on the staircase saw no sign of subsiding anytime soon.

It was time to look for a new office yet again.

| | |

One day in 1983, Bernie called Linda with some exciting news. She had found an empty truck garage on 24th Place in Chinatown and thought it would be perfect for a new CASL office. The garage spanned ten thousand square feet but was in bad shape, with oil-soaked cement floors and an unfinished ceiling of wooden beams. The building would require a complete renovation that would involve putting up drywall, a proper ceiling, and several coats of paint. Before phoning Linda, Bernie had brought it up to the CASL board, and C. W. and Esther were concerned about potential toxins in the building. After an inspection was carried out, the building was deemed safe for renovation and use as a social service agency.

Bernie didn't view this work as an obstacle and instead easily pictured the space divided up among the different departments. She also started to envision how

CASL could expand and bring in new services. Bernie's vision for CASL's new home may have seemed a little idealistic, but it was part of her style—and it was usually successful.

"Bernie never had a master plan," Linda recalled. "She learned as she went. Her personality pushed her to say, 'We need this. We will do this.' She made herself respected and as someone to turn to as a community leader and as someone who worked for the greater community, too. The work Bernie did made the entire Chicago community a better place."

Besides providing more than ten times the amount of space CASL currently occupied, the truck garage seemed ideal to Bernie because, unlike the office on busy Cermak Road, the location of this one was in a residential part of Chinatown that was easier to access for seniors and young families with strollers. There would be no more steep climbing or waiting on the stairs as all of the garage space was on the ground floor. At this time, the residential area north of Cermak had not been developed, so most of CASL's clientele would come from areas south of the Chinatown gate on Wentworth and would not have a far walk or one that involved crossing many busy streets.

Bernie could not stop thinking about the possibilities this new location could give to CASL and the community. She insisted Linda see it for herself, so the two met and investigated this large, brick garage. Linda noticed right away the motor oil–infused floors and the unfinished walls. The garage had obviously suffered through many harsh Chicago winters and damp springs. Yet Linda could also understand how much potential Bernie saw in such a large building. The garage would certainly need a lot of work, which meant CASL would need a lot more money.

CASL still received government, charitable foundation, and corporate funding but nowhere near the half-million dollars needed to buy and renovate the garage. The funds CASL brought in all went to its yearly operating expenses, which continued to increase as CASL offered more and more services.

As the two women stood in the garage and Bernie pointed out her plans for the space, Linda saw another side of her friend. Bernie wasn't just someone who got things done; she was someone who made things happen. Linda appreciated Bernie's excitement but kept thinking about the cost of bringing Bernie's dream to reality. "I suggested raising money for the new office," Linda said.

Bernie's mind sprang into action upon hearing Linda's idea. She immediately thought of a parade through Chinatown with staff, volunteers, and other community members each carrying a broom and cleaning supplies. She relayed her idea to Linda as they continued to stand inside the garage. The parade would start from the street just below their Cermak office, and as they marched through Chinatown, they could collect donations from spectators, ending at the truck garage on 24th Place. And then everyone with a broom could start cleaning up the floor space. Linda could be the leader of the parade.

As fun as that sounded, Linda told Bernie she couldn't imagine raising the money they needed from a street parade. By this time, Linda had already won two Emmy awards for her reporting on the assassination attempt of President Ronald Reagan and for covering a fatal accident at the new State of Illinois Building construction site that killed five workers.[1] She felt her time could be used in more productive ways and suggested a capital campaign to raise enough money to renovate this space, more than just spare change from bystanders along a parade route.

Bernie had no idea how to renovate a truck garage into a thriving social services agency, much less how to raise half a million dollars to make that happen. Even with Linda Yu on her side, these renovations posed a daunting task. But as was typical of her nature, Bernie was undeterred—resolute on doing anything she could to help the Chinatown community—and she forged ahead.

With Linda's assistance, CASL embarked on an eighteen-month capital campaign in January 1984 to raise half a million dollars. It came at a special time in Chicago's history. Harold Washington had just been elected Chicago's first Black mayor the year before and had already reached out to different neighborhoods and communities to bring more representation to city hall. Although his predecessor, Jane Byrne, was not part of the Chicago machine, she was brought into it once she was elected. Washington, on the other hand, broke from the machine and was not accepted by it at all. He faced an uphill battle in city hall because of his race, but that was not going to stop him from working with other underserved communities. Washington wanted a liaison to the Asian American communities in city hall and appointed attorney Paul Igasaki, who would go on to work in the Clinton and Obama administrations at the U.S. Department of Labor and the Equal Employment Opportunity Administration.

But back in the early 1980s, Igasaki got to know Bernie at a Lunar New Year banquet that brought together Chicago's different Asian American communities. This was the first time these communities had all come together, and Igasaki soon invited Bernie to chair an oversight committee at city hall. "Bernie was very committed to having Asian groups all work together," Igasaki recalled, "which was a difficult thing at the time because there were lots of political issues within these

Bernie, second to right, with her mom, Virginia Lo, lower left, and Chicago mayor Harold Washington, second to left. Photo courtesy of Jacinta Wong.

communities. Bernie was very wise and was very politically astute. She wanted to find ways to work as a coalition, not as a competitor."

Although Bernie tried to stay out of politics during the early years of CASL, as she and C. W. had professed to Ping Tom and Wayne Sit, she gladly accepted Igasaki's invitation and already been involved in the 1983 Chicago mayoral elections after Harold Washington won the primary. During the campaign for the general election, Bernie met a young attorney named Tina Tchen, who would go on to serve on the CASL board until she left Chicago decades later to work for the Obama administration. Bernie and Tina Tchen were both involved with Cook County Democratic Women to organize women to become more involved in politics.

CASL also became involved in a national social justice movement in 1982 when a young Chinese American draftsman in Detroit was murdered by two white men. Vincent Chin encountered these men at the Fancy Pants strip club while his friends were throwing him a bachelor party. After Ronald Ebens and Michael Nitz verbally harassed Chin because he was Asian, Chin fought back. It probably wasn't too unusual for fights to break out at a strip club, but bystanders overheard the white men blame Chin for their unemployment. In the early 1980s, the United States and Japanese auto industries were in steep competition for the first time. Since Detroit is the hub of the American auto industry, this rivalry did not go unnoticed. Ebens and Nitz, the two men who picked a fight with Chin, blamed him and thought he represented the Japanese auto industry. They viewed Chin as a foreigner who came to steal their jobs.

Chin and his friends left the club around the same time as Ebens and Nitz, yet the two white men wouldn't let it go and took a baseball bat from their car, chasing Chin and his friends. At first they got away, but after half an hour Ebens and Nitz found Chin. Nitz held down Chin while Ebens beat Chin with the baseball bat. Vincent Chin died from his injuries several days later.

In 1982, there were no hate crime laws and it was difficult for lawmakers and judges to see an anti-Asian hate crime when they didn't experience it themselves. Vincent Chin's murder became a national discussion about identity, hatred, stereotypes, and xenophobia. The following year, Judge Charles Kaufman sentenced Ebens and Nitz to probation and a fine. The judge claimed that the two men had never done anything like this before and that the punishment should fit the criminals, not the crime. Some wondered if Kaufman was prejudiced against Asians after his experience as a World War II prisoner of war by the Japanese military. Although civil rights organizations did not view Vincent Chin's murder as a hate crime, Asian American communities across the country knew better and expressed great outrage at the murder and the sentencing. Bernie decided it was time to showcase CASL as a political voice.

Bernie, third row on the left, against the window, leading a group of Chinatown residents to the Vincent Chin rally in downtown Chicago. The rally would become CASL's first foray into social justice. Photo courtesy of the Chinese American Service League.

In 1983, a number of Asian American organizations organized a protest in downtown Chicago and invited Vincent Chin's mother, Lily. She accepted and traveled to Chicago from her home in Michigan for the rally. As the largest city closest to Detroit—about a six-hour drive—Chicago was a natural place for a rally because of its large and varied Asian American communities.

CASL hired a school bus to bring a group of community members, CASL staff, and Bernie's family downtown. Every seat was occupied. At the rally, CASL joined the Alliance of Asian-Americans of Greater Chicago, an organization of foreign medical graduates, and a group of Filipino Americans, among many others. Mothers stood with their young children, grandmothers with their grown grandchildren, all holding signs that spoke for justice and chastised Judge Kaufman for his miniscule sentence.

Bernie held a sign that read "Probation and a Fine for Killing!" and spent time consoling Lily Chin. The message from Vincent Chin's murder and the trial was that this could have happened to any Asian American and that little, if any, justice would be served. Civil suits were filed later in the 1980s and both Ebens and Nitz were ordered to pay Vincent Chin's estate $1.5 million and $50,000, respectively. Years later, Lily Chin established a scholarship in her son's name.

Although it took another decade for hate crime legislation to pass on a national level, Vincent Chin's murder is still used as an example to show how ignorance and

Bernie, on the right, standing next to Vincent Chin's mother, Lily Chin, at the rally in downtown Chicago calling for justice over the light sentencing of Chin's murderers. Photo courtesy of Jacinta Wong.

xenophobia can turn deadly. This problem has only gotten worse, and although there is awareness of it now, it's difficult to see how much the United States has progressed in fighting anti-Asian hate crimes. It's an issue CASL continues to address today.

| | | |

During the capital campaign for renovations of the new building, the Kresge Foundation offered a matching grant that was followed by other corporate donations. What seemed most special about this capital campaign was that local merchants and residents also donated. Their generous funds proved that CASL was continuing to garner respect in Chinatown and that the community felt that CASL was providing valuable services.

In their annual report from 1985, Bernie and C. W. wrote of the challenges to raise so much money. "The Capital Campaign tested us in areas that we previously had no knowledge in. Understanding and overseeing the renovation at the new facility was both frustrating and rewarding. Fortunately we were able to draw on the resources of a hard working facility committee that was appointed by the Board. The committee has spent hours reviewing drawings and budgets to assure that we get the best for our precious funds."[2]

If CASL could successfully renovate this new office on 24th Place, it could expand the programs it already offered on the second-floor walk-up on Cermak but also reach more members of the community, regardless of age or ability. Refugees continued to come to Chicago; in 1985 alone, CASL helped settle more than 1,200 new arrivals. And resettlement continued to include counseling to help refugees to adjust to their new homes in Chicago, finding jobs, and going through the U.S. immigration process. With more space, CASL staff could see more refugees on any given day.

CASL had been offering ESL classes for several years, but by the middle of the 1980s, it hoped to offer ESL classes with the sole purpose of providing the language skills and subject matter new immigrants would need to go through the U.S. naturalization process. In a later interview with the Chicago Community Trust, Bernie stated, "Our English language classes are essential for all immigrants, and every program is integrated with educating our clients in practical ways to cope with whatever situations arise—like going into a store, understanding American money, using household equipment, and a vast variety of other everyday matters we Americans take for granted."[3]

The new office would also allow CASL to expand its job placement counseling. Finding work is one thing; turning jobs into careers and finding fulfillment are just as important. To help clients stay employed, CASL social workers followed up with the people they placed in jobs to learn if they faced any workplace or commuting issues. When an employee can speak to someone from the outside about their work, job retention is higher and employees are happier, especially when there are language barriers and inevitable misunderstandings. Mike Chan had already shown that counseling helped Vietnamese refugees with job retention. Bernie agreed that it was important to have job counselors work through these issues and for clients to learn skills to build confidence to speak to employers or coworkers.

With a new building, CASL could provide other counseling services for individuals and families. Moving to a new country takes a heavy toll on people responsible for the livelihood of their families. But because counseling was such a new concept for Chinese immigrants, it took a few years for the counseling program at CASL to find acceptance in the community. Soon word got around and CASL social workers started seeing new clients who came to them as referrals from other clients. In the mid-1980s, the *Chicago Tribune* Foundation donated money to start a Young Mothers Literary Program for refugees with young children. The program not only provided English classes but also individual counseling and support groups so Chinese immigrants would not feel alone in their new city.

CASL continued to provide the health screenings it had started in 1980, which by the middle of the 1980s had expanded to include Mercy Hospital and the old Louise Burg Hospital. These screenings were provided to more than three hundred individuals, a 30 percent increase over the previous year.

| | | |

In the early 1980s, CASL also started to offer classes in traditional Chinese arts like dance and music. Obviously, survival skills and confidence were necessary in order to live a fulfilling life, but Bernie and the CASL board were very aware that the arts played an important role in leading a complete life. It may seem frivolous to some that new immigrants and refugees should spend time enjoying the arts instead of focusing on ways to pay their bills, but CASL never saw these areas as mutually exclusive. Bernie and the board viewed them all as ways to find purpose and contentment. After all, China enjoys a rich history of applied and performing arts that go back millennia. If CASL had more space, it could offer dance and music classes to more students.

Just a couple of years after the capital campaign began, a dancer from a professional Chinese dance troupe went to Bernie for advice on immigration and naturalization. Bernie saw an opportunity and hired her to start a cultural and

Bernie and children in the Chinese traditional dance program at CASL to keep new immigrants connected to their families' culture. Photo courtesy of Jacinta Wong.

ethnic dance program that began with thirty children. To fund this program, CASL received a grant from the Chicago Council on Fine Arts. Classes like these allowed children to stay close to their culture and to perform before others, both in Chinatown and at other citywide events.

Capital campaign aside, Bernie did not give up on the broom parade. In 1985, she arranged for more than a hundred marchers to begin a parade in front of CASL's office on Cermak. Many of the participants were teenagers, the boys and girls both with fashionably permed long hair. Regardless of age, the marchers carried brooms while two participants carried a yellow sign with black writing that announced the Chinese American Service League's Parade to Clean a New Center. Bernie marched with a red construction helmet and a wide smile. She was proud of her community and eager to start this new chapter for CASL.

Once the parade reached the truck garage, the participants got to work and started to sweep away the debris on the cracked cement floor, which included paper bags, old wrappings, and other paper scraps. By cleaning the floor, they were preparing the space for renovations to begin.

| | |

Bernie, on the far left next to the car, marching with CASL staff, volunteers, clients, and community members to raise money to renovate the new office on 24th Place. The parade was Bernie's idea and ran from the Cermak Road office to the former truck garage on 24th Place. Photo courtesy of the Chinese American Service League.

After the broom parade, volunteers, staff, and clients helped sweep the inside of the former truck garage in preparation for CASL's new home on 24th Place. Photo courtesy of the Chinese American Service League.

At the end of the eighteen-month capital campaign, CASL reached its goal of half a million dollars. The renovations were able to be completed to give Bernie and her staff more room to serve more people in the community, but the need for more funding had hardly subsided. With more programs and more people in the community coming to CASL for services, Bernie and the board were always looking for ways to meet these needs. As with most nonprofits, money would always be an issue.

In 1987, Linda Yu came up with an idea to raise funds that would allow Bernie and the CASL board to continue to concentrate on CASL's programs and organizational needs. An advisory board could focus solely on fundraising and reaching out to corporate leaders in Chicago to show them that CASL not only helped people in Chinatown but also benefited the city as a whole.

By the mid-1980s, plenty of large corporations based their headquarters in Chicago or the surrounding area. Linda was known and loved all over the Chicago metropolitan area as a favorite anchor on the nightly news. She could reach more people through traditional fundraisers like galas with raffles and auctions than she could parading with brooms through the street. Linda knew that once more corporate leaders met Bernie, they, too, would not be able to say no to her.

In 1989, the advisory board sponsored CASL's first corporate dinner and asked United Airlines CEO Stephen Wolf to chair it. Dr. K. K. Wan, CASL's first landlord in Chinatown, lived in the same condo building as Wolf. "Bernie was so respected that Wolf talked to me about her when we rode the same elevator in our building," Wan remembered. Wan, in turn, thanked Wolf for donating two round-trip tickets from Chicago to Hong Kong to raffle off at a CASL fundraiser. At that time, there were no direct flights from Chicago to Hong Kong and airfare was expensive when compared to the average Chicago salary, not to mention those who earned well below that. So it was a big deal to land two free tickets to Hong Kong as a raffle prize.

The dinner became a tradition that first year, raising $74,000. It was unheard of at the time for an agency of CASL's size and scope to raise such funds in a single evening, especially because it included so much corporate support. Large companies like United Airlines and Sara Lee were more accustomed to sponsoring exhibits at large museums or a season at a nationally renowned theater company or symphony. Investment in an agency like CASL was a testament to all it was providing to the community and to Chicago as a whole. As further evidence of CASL's new profile in the business community, the Sara Lee Foundation in 1991 awarded CASL its Chicago Spirit Award, a sum of $50,000 that is only given to one agency a year. Bernie was also honored that year by United Way of Chicago when she won their Executive of the Year award. It was the first time an Asian American organization had achieved this honor. These relationships and honors would not have been possible without Linda Yu's advisory board and Bernie's outreach to politicians and business leaders in Chicago and beyond.

Linda Yu's advisory board was still going strong at the time of writing and has attracted most of Chicago's Asian American broadcast journalists over the years. Not only did Linda pave the way in her profession for more Asian American reporters and anchors, but she also showed them fulfilling ways to give back to the community. Judy Hsu, anchor at Chicago's ABC Channel 7 at the time of writing, has taken over from Linda as the chair of the advisory board. Apart from a two-year hiatus during the COVID-19 pandemic, the advisory board puts on a $400-a-plate annual spring gala, a more casual fall mixer, and other events to support CASL's programs.

From that first image of people waiting on the stairs, Linda knew Bernie was someone to pay attention to. That meeting started a partnership that would span more than four decades.

8

A Solution to a Very American Problem

Something troubled Bernie in the early 1980s. Throughout Chinatown she saw that young families could not remain together when both parents worked long hours, mainly at Chinese restaurants. Many of these restaurant workers were of child-bearing age and had had children in the United States after they settled into their new lives in Chicago. But it was difficult to work and take care of their children without affordable childcare.

In the mid-1980s, while CASL was renovating the 24th Place garage building, the United States and China had settled into their newly restored diplomatic relations and travel between the two countries was easier than it had been in half a century. The price of a roundtrip plane ticket from Chicago was about the same in the 1980s as it was before the COVID-19 pandemic, around $1,500, and although there were no direct flights to Hong Kong—the closest airline hub to the smaller cities in southern China where most Chinatown residents had family—it was possible to first fly to San Francisco or Los Angeles and then on to Hong Kong. Once parents received their green cards or other visas that would allow them to travel back and forth, the logistics of sending their kids to China for a few years was not difficult as long as they could pay the airfare. On top of this, their U.S.-born children were United States citizens by birth, so there was no problem for them leaving and returning.

For many, this new openness offered a solution to the childcare problem: the children could go to China to stay with their grandparents, sometimes for half a decade until they started kindergarten or first grade. It wasn't optimal, but out of economic necessity it was often the only choice that made sense for parents who worked long hours. American childcare centers are expensive and have a language barrier that is often difficult to navigate. Childcare just wasn't a viable option for most families in Chinatown. And hiring a nanny was usually out of the question because of the cost.

When CASL was incorporated, it set out to work with seniors and teens, but now this need for early childhood services demanded a pivot in a new direction. CASL ran its senior resocialization program and refugee resettlement counseling, but so far, the services for teens were limited to language and culture classes. More programs for teens would have to be put aside for the moment.

A childcare center seemed to be a more pressing need, and if CASL could open one with affordable prices, families in the community would not have to experience such disruption and separation. Bernie knew it was more culturally acceptable for grandparents to care for children and that sending children to a day care center staffed by strangers would seem scary and not worth the worry. But from her own experience living with her family in Hong Kong and from her educational background and work in early childcare services before starting CASL, Bernie felt that the best possible option for healthy family relationships was for children to live with their parents and attend a local, affordable childcare that understood

CASL's new home on 24th Place. This building would serve as CASL's central office and program space for the next two decades. Photo courtesy of the Chinese American Service League.

cultural differences between immigrants and first-generation Americans. A CASL early childcare center would help keep families together.

With the opening of CASL's new 24th Place building in May 1985, the agency would have space to start Chicago's first bilingual Chinese day care center.

| | | |

In the mid-1980s when CASL was renovating the 24th Place garage building and planning for an early childhood center, Bernie had one person in mind to run it. Brenda Chock Arksey had been a teacher of Bernie's daughter, Jacinta, in the 1970s at the First Unitarian Church's preschool at 57th Street and Woodlawn Avenue in Hyde Park. At that time, Brenda was still new to early childhood education, but she eventually earned her master's degree at the renowned Erikson Institute for Early Education. Brenda took classes at the institute's classrooms in the Hyde Park Bank Building not far from the First Unitarian Church.

The Erikson Institute was one of the first graduate schools in the United States to promote the importance of early education in a way that incorporates play and socialization. The institute was also a proponent of Head Start, which Bernie appreciated because of her own work before running CASL. Because of Brenda's educational background, work experience, and understanding of the needs of the Chinese communities in Chicago, Bernie saw her as the perfect person to run CASL's new early childhood program.

Brenda was equally enthusiastic about the program and it didn't take her long to accept Bernie's offer. On October 1, 1985, Brenda was hired to oversee CASL's Childhood Development Center (CDC) and started by filling out early childhood education licensing applications. Thanks to her hard work, when CASL's CDC opened on December 22, 1985, it was licensed to serve two classrooms of twenty children each. Because the converted garage on 24th Place was not a traditional classroom setting, even with the renovations, Brenda purchased rolling cubbies to serve as a divider between the two classrooms.

Before Brenda was hired, Bernie and the CASL board had put together a committee to help plan the CDC. Lucinda Lee Katz, one of the most distinguished early childhood educators in the country, served on this committee. Katz was the first bilingual and bicultural teacher in the San Francisco Public Schools from the late 1960s to early 1970s. She taught at the Erikson Institute, University of Illinois, and University of Chicago and went on to become the long-standing principal of the University of Chicago Laboratory Schools. She also served on the CASL board for more than a decade from the late 1980s until the end of the 1990s. Brenda also helped advise the committee before she started her position, and it became her responsibility to find teachers and students.

The center would be the first in Chinatown to offer full-day childcare, so word got around quickly. A church preschool was already operating in Chinatown, but parents could only choose a few hours in the morning or in the afternoon. If they worked full time, they would have to find other arrangements for the other half of the day. CASL allowed working parents to have a nurturing place for their children to thrive and interact with other kids from early in the morning until the early evening. Chinatown businesses became aware of the center before it opened and promoted it to their employees, many of whom had young children. These employers knew that their employees could work uninterrupted if they didn't have to worry about childcare.

Unlike most preschools in Chicago, Brenda had to think about other multi-cultural and multilingual issues. "There were difficulties when families were split up due to economic hardships," Brenda said. "If children were sent back to China to live with their grandparents, they would only see their parents maybe once a year. When they came back to the U.S. to live with their parents, there were lots of things to overcome like getting to know their parents, language issues, and missing their grandparents." On top of that, if children who knew only Chinese were placed into a group setting that spoke only English, the transition would become even more difficult. So Brenda hired teachers who could speak Cantonese, Toisanese, or Mandarin or a combination of these because the children didn't all know the same Chinese language or dialect. "It was important that they could speak with a teacher who could understand them," Brenda said. "CASL tried to minimize the adjustment."

Brenda also worked hard to advertise the new preschool and to get the word out in Chinatown. "I passed out flyers and talked to churches, benevolent associations, and the Chinatown Chamber of Commerce," Brenda recalled. "Businesses knew that their employees would now have a childcare option and could bring their children back to the U.S. from China."

But because CASL's early childhood program was the first in Chinatown, it could not accept every applicant when it opened. There just wasn't enough space. So CASL decided that applicants had to be from low-income families who would pay for preschool according to a sliding scale based on parents' salaries. CASL believed those families needed help the most because childcare was prohibitively expensive and otherwise unobtainable to them.

This criterion did not go over well with some Chinatown families. Middle-class parents found it to be unfair and openly criticized CASL for excluding their

An end-of-the-year celebration in 1987 for the first group of students at CASL's preschool. The photo was taken inside the 24th Place former truck garage. Photo courtesy of the Chinese American Service League.

children. After all, they also deserved full-time childcare. Even though they were in the middle class, they couldn't always afford or find good childcare, especially in a Chinese cultural setting. But forty spots was not a lot and CASL had to draw a line somewhere, even though close to one hundred children would go on the waitlist.

Yet once children were accepted into the program, the parents found that they did not quite understand how their children were being taught. In immigrant families, education is often viewed as the only way to succeed. From their experiences in China, they saw teaching as rote learning, repeating and reciting what was supposed to be learned. When immigrant parents saw their children were receiving an education at CASL that was not similar to their own, they feared their children would not succeed and would be unable to find a job that steadily put food on the table and paid the bills.

In the United States, on the other hand, experiential learning was an approach to early education that allowed children to learn and discover at their pace, using their interests as a starting point. Teachers guided students in all areas of development: cognitive, language, social, emotional, physical and fine motor development. And these in turn fostered the students' social-emotional development and helped them to share with other students and work together in groups. "CASL had to balance two approaches to education: the experientially based American/Montessori approach and the rote/repetition-based approach that Chinese immigrant families understood. It was always a tough balance between the two, which was revisited with new immigrant families," Brenda said many years after the preschool opened.

Since the majority of children in the CDC spoke Chinese at home, the center offered a Chinese-English bilingual curriculum to develop children's language and literary skills in two languages, which included books and music from both cultures.

Teachers were mindful to make sure the parents felt heard and understood, so they emphasized where each child was in each stage of their development and their acquisition of social and language skills. At the same time, teachers also were addressing the parents' academic-based questions.

"If the parents asked what their children learned, the teachers would say they learned colors, not from worksheets but through experiential play, for example color matching games, stories, and music. We learned best practices from the Erikson Institute and would try to help parents understand their children's developmental level," Brenda recalled. CASL assessed the children on a quarterly basis and met with parents periodically to discuss their children's individual progress. The parents seemed pleased with these reports.

| | |

Head Start partially funded the CASL center and stipulated that certain forms of rote learning—for example, worksheets—were not permitted. Head Start money was especially important because it required teachers to achieve certain educational requirements and for childcare centers to pay their staff according to a certain salary scale. Head Start would help pay for teachers' salaries and educational requirements.

The CASL center also received funding from the state for families that could not afford the costs of quality care. For example, the Preschool for All program required teachers to have a certain level of credentials and Child Care funding required basic licensing standards. All of these funding sources allowed CASL to raise the quality of its services.

Teachers at the center have master's degrees in early childhood education and have a strong understanding of how children develop and construct knowledge, so they are able to design their lesson plans to fit the needs of the wide range of abilities of two- to five-year-olds. And they construct their curriculum in ways that are relevant to the individual child's interests and experiences. Eventually, CASL was able to hire a full-time social worker and a part-time nurse for the preschool. The center received accreditation by the National Association for the Education of Young Children in the early 1990s and is still accredited to this day.

Brenda and her teachers tried their best, which became apparent when the children demonstrated how well prepared they were for kindergarten. Because of this preparation, most parents usually came around to the play-based methods. But sometimes to appease parents when they still seemed concerned, Brenda and the other teachers gave the children worksheets only after these skills had become second nature to the children. It also didn't go unnoticed when shy or resistant children started to share and interact well with their classmates.

The preschool was also fortunate to have help from Elaine Wong, wife of longtime CASL board president Art Wong. Elaine was a psychiatrist who had her own private practice and was also a dedicated CASL volunteer. She served on the preschool's advisory committee and volunteered as a child psychologist consultant for fifteen years. She would hold monthly consultations with CASL staff, and because she didn't speak Chinese, Esther would serve as her interpreter at each meeting. The benefit of a child psychologist was immense and the CASL staff could regularly run their concerns by Elaine.

Although now with an increasing number of full-time preschools in Chinatown, CASL's has remained one of the strongest and most popular programs at the agency. "CDC's education program is developmentally appropriate because we meet the children where they are, both individually and as a group, and because we use our assessment tools to provide challenging and achievable goals for each child," Brenda said.

9
Have You Eaten?

Although many new immigrants felt most comfortable living and working in Chinatown, the wages and working conditions there were not always comparable to those found in jobs downtown. Bernie recognized this and felt it important to offer skills to immigrants and other Chinatown residents that would allow them to find work beyond Wentworth and Cermak. Mike Chan, in his role as a social worker, had helped place Vietnamese refugees in hotel housekeeping jobs at the Ambassador East Hotel with union benefits. There was no reason Chinatown residents couldn't also find jobs in better-paying Chicago establishments, including some of the poshest restaurant kitchens. Yet to work in a Western restaurant, someone would need to know something as simple as setting a table.

CASL started a basic table manners class to provide these skills. This class became so popular that it soon changed into something much larger that would impact not just Chinatown residents but Chicago as a whole.

Soon after the new 24th Place building opened, CASL started two culinary programs that developed from the table setting class: pastry/baking and chef training. The thought was that graduates of the former program could find work in bakeries and at restaurants, while people who completed the latter could work in any capacity in a Western restaurant kitchen.

In true CASL fashion, the first sixty graduates were not left to find work on their own after they finished the program. CASL had hired job counselors specifically for this program to connect with hotels and restaurants around the city. The timing was fortuitous, as was the case with many CASL programs. In 1978, brothers Larry and Mark Levy opened a restaurant in Chicago's Water Tower Place that would grow into the billion-dollar Levy Restaurants group. The company now runs restaurants at some of Chicago area's most scenic locations, such as along the Chicago River and at the Ravinia Festival. It also caters many of the leading sports arenas around the country. Seven years before Levy Restaurants started, Rich Melman and Jerry Orzoff opened their own restaurant in Chicago's Lincoln Park neighborhood that would spark the multimillion-dollar Lettuce Entertain You group with eateries of different cuisines, also spread across the country.

When CASL started its culinary program, Bernie was already familiar with Mark Levy and Rich Melman and tapped into these connections when it came time to place graduates in restaurant jobs around Chicago.

The sixteen-week Chef Training Program began in 1986 and followed a comprehensive schedule for eight hours each day. It soon changed into one program covering both food preparation and pastry making. At eight o'clock in the morning, students would review their textbook reading assignments and discuss that day's recipe with their instructors. An interpreter helped translate from the instructors' English to the students' Chinese dialects. At nine o'clock, the students would prepare the recipe they had just discussed. Using skills they had read about in the textbook the night before, the students would work on new techniques such as how to make hollandaise sauce. Lunch took place between noon and one o'clock and the students would eat what they had just prepared. Their work was judged by Bernie and two of her closest colleagues.

Ricky Lam was CASL's Employment and Training Department manager and helped sample the students' creations each day, along with Bernie and Monica Tang, an employment and vocational training counselor who first started as Bernie's assistant. The three would offer honest feedback on taste, texture, and color. During the following hour, between one and two o'clock, the students would clean their workstations and rest up.

For the last two hours of the day, students would learn English from Louis Chan, the staff member who served as an interpreter in their program. The fact that ESL was 25 percent of the day was a reflection of the program's emphasis on English as a Second Language. Chan would teach the students the English vocabulary they would find in that evening's textbook assignment, as well as the terms of techniques and ingredients they had worked with that day. Chan would also practice interview skills with the students, all in English. Before students left at the end of the day, Chan would assign their reading for that evening and introduce the recipe for the following day.

Monica and the chefs once brought a group of trainees to Spiaggia, one of Chicago's top restaurants at the time, part of Levy Restaurants, and a favorite of Barack and Michelle Obama when they lived in Chicago. The students not only met with Spiaggia's head chef, but many were hired on the spot. Students also attended the National Restaurant Association week at the McCormick Place convention center in Chicago. For many, it was their first time at McCormick Place and opened their eyes to a culinary world outside of Chinatown.

Graduates of the Chef Training Program have gone on to find fulfilling careers at top Chicago hotels, jobs that have provided them with living wages, medical insurance, union membership, and paid vacation. Some found work at Café Bernard and the Halsted Street Fishmarket, both owned by Sue Ling Gin, an entrepreneur, CASL board member, and major CASL donor. Gin was also the CEO of Flying Food Fare, an airline catering company that started making meals for Midway Airlines and went on to secure deals with British Airways, Air France-KLM, Qantas, and Royal Jordanian. Graduates of the program were hired en masse at Flying Food Fare, which became one of the most sought-after employers in the CASL job placement program.

In more recent years, the Langham Hotel has hired a CASL graduate as a sous chef and the Hilton Chicago found its executive pastry chef from the CASL program. Another graduate is a sous chef at the Peninsula Hotel's Shanghai Terrace, the most high-end Chinese restaurant in Chicago.

While many graduates have gone on to Western restaurants and five-star hotels, some have returned to Chinatown to give back to the community. The program is still going strong and enjoys more than a 90 percent rate of successfully placing graduates in full-time culinary jobs with benefits and wages on which they and their families can live.

Soon after the Chef Training Program commenced, a young man named Kenneth Tsang moved to Chicago from Hong Kong. He enrolled in the program and met Eileen, also from Hong Kong and the woman who would become his wife. It was difficult to pick up and move to another country, but Kenneth and Eileen were both eager to learn new skills that could give them a comfortable life in Chicago. The two looked forward to meeting up at eight o'clock each morning to begin class. As their daughter Anna recounted years later, "My parents learned how to cut, slice, and prepare food, set the table, and provide customer service. As part of the program, they had English classes every day to help them assimilate into the American workforce." When Eileen graduated, she gave a speech in English—for the first time—at the banquet held in honor of her class.

Through CASL's employment matching program, Eileen found a job at Spiaggia and Kenneth was hired at the Chicago Baking Company. After working in their respective jobs for a few years, Kenneth and Eileen were able to save enough money

A class of the chef training program putting their skills to use at an event in Chicago.
Photo courtesy of the Chinese American Service League.

to start their own bakery in Chinatown, which they named Saint Anna Bakery
and Café. They rented space in the then-new retail development at Chinatown
Square on Archer.

At the time, there were not many Hong Kong–style bakeries in Chicago and
the Tsangs wanted to share this special East-meets-West cuisine. Famous for their
chestnut cakes and white chocolate mousse cakes not found in other Chinatown
bakeries, Saint Anna would fill its large glass display case with these and other
pastries, which became the focal point of their café. Also in the display case were
individually cut slices of Western cakes layered with whipped cream and slices
of fresh fruit that stood next to delicate Chinese egg tarts, fluffy barbecued pork
buns, and glutinous rice balls filled with red bean paste.

For diners who preferred savory food, the bakery offered a menu of rice dishes
and noodle soups. It wasn't unusual for friends to congregate at Saint Anna for
hours, drinking Hong Kong milk tea with a Chinese pastry or piece of Western
cake or enjoying a hot bowl of noodles for breakfast or lunch. The café quickly
became a favorite eatery in Chinatown.

"My parents kept a close relationship with Bernie and the CASL organization
even after they had parted from the culinary and restaurant job-match program.
They bought fundraiser tickets and gifted cakes for CASL events," Anna Tsang

said. She also spent time at CASL, learning Chinese art and dance in the after-school programs. Anna recalls fondly, "CASL referred me to a youth sustainability internship that had a lasting impact on me. I later graduated with a BS degree in environmental economics." Her sister Erica attended CASL's day care program and later in high school tutored immigrants to help them prepare for their citizenship exams. Anna and Erica's grandmother also took citizenship preparation classes at CASL and a cousin met his wife while volunteering at the agency.

Kenneth and Eileen eventually sold Saint Anna and moved out west. "CASL is so valuable and necessary in the Chinese community," Anna said. "My family and I will continue to stay connected and give back even now when we have moved out of Chicago to the West Coast." The bakery and their legacy remain in Chinatown as of this writing and is still a beloved café in the area. Their story is just one of many that have helped new immigrants find meaningful careers in Chicago.

10

The Next Generation of Social Workers

Although the CMAA was running strong in Uptown by 1986, CASL still served some clients in this Chicago neighborhood known for its Vietnamese community. Shing Lee had been counseling Vietnamese refugees for a number of years, but by 1986 he had been promoted to the office manager of the new 24th Place office to help Bernie with administrative work. With Lee's departure from the northside, CASL briefly opened an office in Uptown to continue to help its clients in this neighborhood.

Yung Chan was a thirty-year-old Hong Kong social worker who moved to Chicago as a newlywed in 1985. Like many Chinese immigrants in Chicago, Chan had heard about CASL from word of mouth and sought out a meeting with Bernie to see what type of job opportunities were available for someone with her skills.

When Bernie learned of Chan's social work background, she wasted no time making an offer to hire her full time. Chan was sent Uptown and recalled years later, "I was initially entrusted primarily to a Vietnamese refugee project and counselling services for Chinese newcomers and residents. I visited clients, explored services, liaised with resource providers, and rendered supportive help to those in livelihood hardship. Being a fresh alien myself, I was compelled to learn fast, adjust speedily, and render help to clients with poise despite my own initial inadequacies."[1]

Along with Chan, this Uptown office was staffed with Anh Truong, another CASL employee who was fluent in Vietnamese, and Monica Tang, Bernie's former assistant. The women provided job counseling and spoke to the refugees about American workplace culture. But as CASL's programs grew in Chinatown and the demand for services there continued to increase, there didn't seem to be

Left to right: Anh Truong, Yung Chan, and Monica Tang with a client at CASL's Uptown office. Photo courtesy of Jacinta Wong.

a compelling reason for the agency to remain in Uptown. In hindsight, there probably wasn't much point in opening an Uptown office after Shing Lee was promoted since CMAA was already well established in the area. CASL closed its Uptown office not too long after it opened.

| | |

A year later, in 1987, the Chicago Public Schools (CPS) made national news with a three-week teacher's strike that fall. Harold Washington was mayor and felt deeply invested not only in getting teachers back in the classrooms but also in introducing reforms that would help solve the issues that brought the teachers to strike in the first place. After the strike concluded, Washington spoke with one thousand parents and, from there, put together a task force of fifty parents and community leaders who would organize meetings in their neighborhoods to discuss the problems specific to their schools.

The mayor's reforms were not taken so well by U.S. secretary of education William Bennett in the Reagan administration. When Bennett got wind of the changes underway at CPS, he traveled to Illinois where he loudly stated that

Chicago's public school system was the worst in the country. "If it's not the last, I don't know who is. There can't be very many more cities that are worse. Chicago is pretty much it."[2] Bennett attributed CPS's problems to a large bureaucracy at the Chicago Board of Education.

Harold Washington took offense and knew that the Reagan administration often demonized Chicago when it wasn't warranted. "Mr. Bennett has a lot of gall to be criticizing Chicago Public Schools or any other school system . . . in light of the fact that he's employed by Ronald Reagan, who has literally dismantled public education in this country."[3] Besides cutting the bureaucracy, Bennett suggested a controversial solution: vouchers.

The concept and discussion of school vouchers had been ongoing for years. Under a voucher system, families would receive government vouchers—funded by tax-payer dollars—to enroll their children in a public or private school of their choice. Thus, a large portion of federal funds for public education could land in the hands of private schools and away from public schools, making it very difficult for the latter to survive. On top of that, the possibility of low-income students enrolling in a private school is often next to impossible due to transportation logistics and other expenses that are not covered by the vouchers. Vouchers are still a controversial topic today because they are designed to give middle-class and high-income students choices while keeping low-income students down.

Harold Washington recognized that CPS had many problems and faced great challenges but not from the bureaucracy to which Bennett pointed. Instead, these issues stemmed from the pockets of poverty that results from the inequity between different neighborhoods. After his task force met with members of their own neighborhoods, they reported back to him.

These conversations resulted in the mayor's new initiative, the 1988 Chicago School Reform Act, which stipulated that a Local School Council (LSC) be established for each public school in the CPS system. It was the hope that LSCs would improve neighborhood schools by engaging parents and community members of the area that fed into these schools. Instead of relying on the centralized Chicago Board of Education to make decisions for local schools, the LSCs could figure out for themselves what they needed. LSCs also recruited, hired, and reviewed their principals' contracts. They managed their schools' budgets and provided input on the curriculum. For instance, an LSC could allow a school in Chinatown to include a bilingual program to maintain Chinese-language abilities and ESL teachers to work with new immigrants. LSC representatives are elected by the community and it isn't necessary to be a U.S. citizen to vote in an LSC election. Likewise, those running for an LSC position do not need to be U.S. citizens, obtain a certain level of education, or even be employed. They just need to have an interest in their community and be able to put in the time to attend the meetings. In other words, LSCs were open to people who may not normally be involved in political decision-making.

LSCs also had another effect on their communities. It would be difficult for parents and other members of the community to ignore problems in the schools if they took a more active role in how their schools ran and saw how their schools fit into their communities. Although this structure of grassroots engagement may sound like a commonsense plan, the road to establishing the LSCs turned out to be a long and arduous one.

Each school in the CPS system was not equal to the others. Some provided excellent education and extracurricular resources while others did not have school libraries or basic supplies. In the poorest neighborhoods, high rates of crime made it dangerous for students to even reach school each morning. And if they could get to school, there was always the walk home to worry about. There was much to fix.

Each LSC was made up of a number of people: the school's principal, two teachers, six parents, two community members, and a student for high schools.

CASL became involved in recruiting members of the Chinese community to run for local school councils, a newly established entity thanks to reforms enacted by Mayor Harold Washington. The LSCs gave communities more say in their neighborhood schools. Photo courtesy of the Chinese American Service League.

So in 1989, Bernie hired a newly graduated social worker named Catalina Chan to work on the School Reform Project, Harold Washington's initiative that came from the 1988 Chicago School Reform Act. Catalina was tasked with motivating Chinatown residents to become involved with their local schools, namely by joining an LSC. "It was a reformative and empowerment project to improve the public school system in Chicago," Catalina recalled.

As Catalina spoke with members in the Chinese community, she introduced them to the concept of the LSC and explained the benefits of participating in the CPS system at a very local level. With more community involvement, more connections could be built between the schools and the people who lived around them. And because LSCs met at their schools, community members would never need to travel very far for meetings. These meetings were usually held in the early evening, well after the workday ended but not too late that it would turn away potential members.

All of these factors—the ease in getting to meetings, the benefits to both the schools and community, and the rewards of participating in a local government body—started to sound good to the people Catalina spoke with. By her third year at CASL, she was able to recruit a few members of the Chinese community into three different LSCs. Thanks to her hard work, the Chinese community enjoyed more representation and input in the CPS. "The project won the Chicago Spirit Award in 1992," Catalina recalled.

She would work at CASL for five years, from 1989 to 1994, and recalled this time fondly. "During the significant developmental stage of CASL, my work was tremendous, stressful, and encountered different competition with other communities. Bernie gave me a lot of trust and autonomy. She was very positive and encouraging. Bernie was like the commander who had faith in her troops and made things possible." After Catalina left CASL, she continued her social work career for another thirty years. "I am proud and glad to have learned from Bernie in my first few years as a social worker. All her characteristics influenced me deeply."[4]

Catalina's contributions to the Chinatown community cannot be understated. She brought encouragement and new opportunities to residents when it came to public education in Chicago. There is no greater investment in a community than in its public education.

11

The Zhou Brothers Plant Roots in Chicago

In Mandarin, there is a saying, *huxiang bangzhu* 互相幫助, which translates to helping each other in a way that mutually benefits both parties. Sometimes CASL's greatest achievements came not from a perceived need in the community but a chance opportunity that enriched the Chinatown community and Chicago as a whole. One of the most striking examples of this is when the Zhou brothers arrived in Chicago from China in the mid-1980s.

The brothers were born in the 1950s to booksellers in Guangxi Province. Their province borders both China's Guangdong Province and Vietnam, the birthplaces of many CASL clients and Chinese residents in Chicago. Now known as ShanZuo and DaHuang Zhou, the brothers were raised by their grandmother, a nurturing woman who fostered their love of painting from an early age.

As adults, the brothers painted in an old warehouse, not unlike the truck garage Bernie found for CASL in the mid-1980s. Around the time the new CASL building opened on 24th Place, ShanZuo and DaHuang Zhou arrived in Chicago. It was 1986 and as they recalled, "We made our long way from China to Chicago carrying a box of artwork and thirty American dollars with the ambition to impress the world with our art. Chicago in the 1980s was already a world-class city with modern high-rise buildings. With its fame in the diversity in architecture styles, Chicago is prestigiously known as a modern architecture museum."[1]

At that time, there weren't many opportunities in China for contemporary artists like the Zhous. It had been a decade since the end of the Cultural Revolution and China was still rebuilding after decades of hardship. So the brothers picked Chicago for its architecture, art museums, and the outdoor public sculpture—including works by Picasso, Miró, and Calder—for which the city is renowned.

"Since 1984, an annual international art exhibition has been held at Chicago's Navy Pier," the brothers said in a statement. "It was the most important art exhibition in the world at that time. Chicago's sense of modernity and the embracement of diversity made us intuitively feel that this city would play a crucial role in the field of modern art. That was why we decided to settle in Chicago."

Even though they had experienced their fair share of cold winters in China, the brothers still felt the shock of Chicago's frigid months. "Yet the decision to relocate imposed a great challenge on our lives. We didn't know English well. We had no friends in Chicago who could help us. It started snowing in Chicago in November that first year. Lake Michigan turned to a huge ice rink at -20°C, which looked astonishing. The winter coats we bought from Beijing, which looked like military ones, obviously were not enough to keep us warm. In addition to adapting to an unfamiliar place, these all posed a great challenge."

After they arrived in Chicago, they felt fortunate to connect with another artist, Haishao Chen, who knew Bernie and the work she did at CASL. Chen thought it would be worthwhile for the brothers to meet her, so he made that introduction. "It was spring 1987 when the snow gradually melted and the tulips by Lake Michigan began to bud," the brothers recalled. "We had already heard of the good name of CASL as a charity organization that assists Chinese immigrants in various aspects of life, including language, job prospects, medical services, etc. They have helped many Chinese immigrants fulfill their American dream. We longed to meet Bernie."

And when Bernie learned of their talent, her mind immediately went to CASL's emerging arts programs. Bernie could not let this special opportunity pass and quickly enlisted the brothers to teach a painting class at the new CASL center on 24th Place. Two weeks later, CASL offered its first art class. "Since then, we have forged an indissoluble bond and deep friendship with Bernie," the brothers said.

Yet Bernie did not want to hold the brothers down at CASL and sought ways to help them find more opportunities to showcase their work. Just a decade earlier, the city's central library building on Michigan Avenue had been converted into the Chicago Cultural Center, a free venue for visual and performing arts. In 1988, Bernie helped the Zhou brothers arrange an exhibit of their work there. "We decided to donate these works to CASL," the brothers recalled. "All the sales profit made were spent on serving the community. Bernie Wong's broad mind and love has influenced everyone around her, leading to further betterment and growth of CASL."

The Zhou Brothers working with students at their CASL drawing class. Cultural arts classes are important to CASL because they allow children and adults to remain connected to their culture. Photo courtesy of Jacinta Wong.

From this show, the brothers discovered a new style of oil painting that focused on mixing various materials that would become their trademark for the next decade.

CASL also helped them apply for permanent residency, and Bernie put in a good word with A. D. Moyer, the district director of U.S. Immigration and Naturalization office in Chicago. They were successful on their first attempt and have since become internationally acclaimed artists known as the Zhou Brothers.

The Chicago art scene would change with the arrival of the Zhou Brothers. They not only helped Chinatown residents learn about art, but today they provide studio space for dozens of local artists at the Zhou B Art Center, which also has a first-floor museum space and bookstore. It's located at the old Spiegel Catalog Building in the Bridgeport neighborhood, adjacent to Chinatown, and has become a sought-after wedding venue and fundraising event space. For two decades, CASL and the Zhou B Art Center have partnered for fundraising events.

To commemorate Bernie's legacy in Chinatown, the Zhou Brothers created a sculpture dedicated to Bernie, titled *Red Angel*, in October 2021 and unveiled it across from CASL's current building on Tan Court. The space where the sculpture stands was designed by longtime CASL board member Ernie Wong, also the developer of Ping Tom Park.

The Red Angel sculpture from the Zhou Brothers, dedicated in memory of Bernie Wong, October 2021. Photo courtesy of the author.

The plaque on *Red Angel* reads:

Dedicated to the memory of Bernarda Lo Wong, Co-founder of the Chinese American Service League in 1978, the Red Angel sculpture by the internationally acclaimed Zhou Brothers watches over the Chinatown Community. Her devotion to the community illuminated Chicago's Chinatown across the world. Her contributions to social work and her accomplishments in community service brought accolades from around the globe. Her spirit of the Red Angel symbolizes the hope and perseverance of Chicago's Asian American Community.

The Zhou Brothers look back fondly on their collaboration with Bernie and CASL in a written statement: "During these 30-plus years, we often sat by the vine frame full of violets in the sculpture garden of our Chicago studio to listen to Bernie Wong's ideas for the prospects of CASL. She was always so enthusiastic, kind, and passionate. She rarely talked about her family and herself. Forty years are almost more than half of a person's life. How great Bernie Wong was to selflessly devote forty years of precious energy, love, passion, and faith to this community, the charity, and Chicagoland."

PART III

The Expansive 1990s

12

The Youth Center on Canal Street

CASL's early plans for teen outreach seemed to have taken a back seat for the agency's first dozen years. Unforeseen needs like refugee resettlement and childcare popped up, as did new opportunities to apply for grants in these areas. But Bernie and the CASL board still hoped to help Chinatown teens.

To outsiders, Chinatown teens may not have seemed in need of after-school services or a place to go when school wasn't in session. Why couldn't these teens just go home after school and do homework or stay at home on their days off? It wasn't that simple.

For decades, Asian Americans have been labeled the "model minority" by others in the United States, a label that is not only incorrect but also ignores the same issues that other communities face across the country. It's natural for parents to worry about the lure of vice when it comes to their teenagers, just as Bernie's mother had done when Bernie was applying to colleges in the United States. As with teens across the country, some in Chinatown could focus on school and part-time jobs while others rebelled by staying out late at night, skipping school, or even joining a street gang.

With Childcare School Age funding, CASL sought to expand its children's program to include services for elementary school children. In August 1990, a new program, School Age Center, was established for first through fourth graders. Twenty-seven students enrolled that year and received homework tutoring and cultural arts classes. CASL also held a three-day camp for twenty-eight teens and preteens to learn about the dangers of substance abuse.

One of the joys of living in Chicago is the exposure to other cultures and backgrounds, and the CASL staff was very aware of the importance of feeling comfortable around people from other backgrounds. So the after-school program also brought students outside Chinatown to the Field Museum where they learned about African instruments and to the Ukrainian Museum on Chicago's northside. Parents in the community appreciated these new after-school options for their grade school children. Yet that still left teens with no place to go after school. To finally be able to serve this age group, Bernie and the board knew that they would need more space.

But as with the 24th Place truck garage, new space could not be obtained without more money. In 1990, the board approved another capital campaign to establish a dedicated youth center that would be housed separate from the 24th Place building. There was no way CASL's current building could accommodate more students, even if it was mostly in the hours after school.

That year, CASL applied for a grant of $64,000 from United Way of Chicago and $60,000 from the Chicago Community Trust, to be given over three years to start a more substantial after-school program. The Metropolitan YMCA of Chicago also helped CASL with program development and opened its facilities at the New City YMCA on the northside so children in CASL's programs could use their swimming pool and gymnasium. On top of that, the International YMCA connected with the Hong Kong YMCA to send a youth counselor from Hong Kong to Chicago for six months to help CASL develop its new Teen Reach Program. The YMCA would pay for the Hong Kong youth counselor's salary and expenses. CASL also started a Boy Scout program at this time.

All these donations and grants were difficult to keep track of and Bernie knew there would be even more donations and grants in the future as CASL started its second full decade of operations. It was time to start an accounting program. Bernie's previous assistant, Monica Tang, who later served as employment and vocational counselor with the Chef Training Program, stepped up to take on this new responsibility. In 1989, Jerry Erickson, the head of United Charities Chicago, who had donated the first office space to Bernie at his downtown Chicago office back in 1978, asked his accountant to train Monica to establish an accounting department at CASL. To do this, CASL purchased and installed a computer hardware and software system for financial planning and reporting, becoming fully self-sufficient in managing its finances.

By 1991, Monica was the accounting manager and was working with a $1.2 million budget. A decade later, in 2002, she would become CASL's comptroller. "I took pride in establishing CASL's accounting department," Monica said. Her rise up the career ladder, from assistant to job counselor to accounting manager and finally to comptroller was a testament to the opportunities Bernie and the CASL board provided to members of the CASL family, "despite all the endless evenings and weekends," according to Monica, that came with working for the agency.

Bernie could not stop thinking about the key question involved with opening a new youth center: location. There didn't seem to be a building with adequate space near the 24th Place center. Kids needed room to run around, especially after a long day at school or during Chicago's frigid winters. So it was a great challenge to find a building that would provide adequate space. In this instance, raising money was not the most pressing challenge, thanks to Linda Yu's advisory board and the annual corporate fundraisers. By early 1991, CASL had raised an additional $120,000 for a new youth center.

Not long after that, a 9,700-square-foot building at 2326 South Canal Street became available just on the outskirts of Chinatown. It seemed like the perfect place for CASL's new youth center. With the addition of this building, CASL's workable space almost doubled. It was a far cry from Dr. Wan's free storage room or the second-floor offices on Cermak that Linda Yu first saw when she and her cameraperson trekked up the staircase as dozens of clients patiently waited to meet with Bernie.

The Children and Youth Center opened in April 1991 and was able to meet the needs of low-to-moderate-income school-aged children. There weren't other after-school programs in Chinatown at that time that provided homework tutoring and recreational activities. CASL's School Age Program served kids aged six to twelve so parents wouldn't have to worry about their children returning to an empty house after school.

Organized gang activity in Chinatown dropped significantly after a 1988 Federal Bureau of Investigation (FBI) bust at the On Leong Chinese Merchants Association, yet teenage street gangs still posed a threat to susceptible kids. With the new youth center now up and running, Bernie and the CASL board felt it was time to find ways to engage preteens and teens in ways that would keep them from the temptations of easy money and quick companionship. In the early 1990s, CASL was finally able to fill a crucial missing piece in their services and start a teen drop-in program for middle school and high school students to have a place to work on homework, receive tutoring, or just hang out with friends. CASL has always relied on volunteers and the youth center was no exception. Teens from the area volunteered to tutor younger kids. Herman So, the boy Bernie helped when his mother was dying of lung cancer, became one of these essential volunteers during his high school years but before the youth center was open.

CASL opened its Youth Center on Canal Street in 1991 and would use this space for the next decade until all of the programs could be housed in the new building on Tan Court. Photo courtesy of the Chinese American Service League.

These services began none too soon as Chinatown and the adjacent Bridgeport neighborhood both saw a rapid increase in new immigrants in the early 1990s as more people from China were able to move abroad. In 1991 alone, more than 1,300 children and teens participated in CASL youth programs, which included the teen drop-in center, fine and performing arts classes, family and individual counseling, and sports and recreational activities.

| | | |

In 1991, CASL identified another group that would benefit from a program that brought them together. Young families with stay-at-home parents and caregivers with younger children had few ways of connecting in Chinatown unless they happened to meet as neighbors or at a park. In affluent areas of the city, parents and caregivers had a wide range of playgroups and classes tailored for infants and toddlers before they reached the age to start preschool. If Chinatown parents wanted to attend these programs, they would have to leave their area and go to another part of Chicago where they most likely would have language difficulties.

Besides a lack of parent-tot classes, young parents in Chinatown at that time often didn't have their own parents or other relatives in the Chicago area. They had few resources to turn to when they needed support in the unforeseen demands of parenthood or wanted information about finding a short-term babysitter. To bring these families together, in the summer of 1990, CASL started a summer pilot Early Childhood Program, partially funded by the Chicago Board of Education. This Family Fun Club organized trips to parks and museums around Chicago that were outside of Chinatown. This opened up the city to these young families, who then made connections with others in the group that came from similar backgrounds.

The summer pilot showed that there was a greater need beyond a support group for young families. CASL looked at Family Focus in Chicago and Wu Yee in San Francisco and felt it, too, could bring parents, caregivers, and children together to help children and families grow and develop in their new American environment. So the following year, CASL started a new program: the Family Learning and Resource Center (FALREC). "It was a home away from home," Brenda Arksey explained, "especially for young mothers without a support system here. They could go there with their infants and toddlers to meet other families and develop a support system, like a surrogate family." FALREC became a family support program that embraced their children, parents, and extended families.

Yet FALREC did not just provide these families with a place to gather but included play groups, parent workshops, and recreational activities. In addition, there was a library and resource center with materials on child-rearing and the adjustments new immigrants face in the United States, as well as a parents' lounge and children's playroom. Funding for FALREC started with a three-year grant from the John D. and Catherine T. MacArthur Foundation.

If FALREC families needed babysitters or wanted to meet others who spoke the same language or understood the same cultural challenges they faced in Chicago, they suddenly had more options through the families they met at CASL. FALREC also arranged field trips to other parts of Chicago and to the suburbs so parents could experience new areas without worrying about finding their own way at first. If they didn't drive—and many didn't—or take the bus, sometimes these field trips were the first time FALREC participants had left Chinatown.

FALREC also provided home visits, including supporting young families in their home environment and in-home early intervention assessments to check for the possibilities of developmental delays—for example, speech and motor skill delays. By law, Illinois provides speech and occupational therapists in an in-home setting for children under three, so CASL's Prevention Initiative Program under the FALREC umbrella provided these services.

The three programs—Child Development Center, School Age Center, and FALREC—together built a strong foundation from which CASL provided a multitude of services for the community, from infancy to senior services. Children

Esther Wong presides over the dedication of the Vernon Sandacz Children and Youth Center. Sandacz was a CASL board member and social worker who dedicated his life to helping children. Photo courtesy of the Chinese American Service League.

grew up at CASL as some started from infancy and followed through the youth programs into college and jobs. Both the Child Development Center and School Age Center became accredited and maintained excellent national standards of quality programming. Most of the participants in these programs came from two-parent working families. As Brenda recalled, "There were some students who came from single-parent families, but that would become more prevalent later on." Now CASL serves many more single-parent families because divorce in the United States and China is much more prevalent than it was forty years ago.

| | | |

In the mid-1990s, the youth center was renamed the Vernon Sandacz Children and Youth Center after longtime board member Vern Sandacz suddenly passed away in 1995. Sandacz was a social worker dedicated to helping underserved children and his contributions to CASL were invaluable. In memory of his legacy, CASL dedicated the youth center in his name and would continue to do so until the early 2000s when CASL faced yet another challenge with providing enough space for the programs it wanted to offer.

13

Expanding Senior Services

As much as childcare was a top priority, Bernie and the CASL board never lost sight of their original commitment to seniors. When the 24th Place office opened, CASL was already providing seniors with counseling and health screenings as well as social programs like an annual camping trip and arts and crafts classes. Its Chore Service Program, which began in 1980, reached two dozen homebound seniors who had trouble with mobility and could not easily move about their homes. CASL sent part-time staff to help these seniors with basic housekeeping tasks like dusting and cleaning bathrooms and kitchens. Aides also bought groceries for these seniors and made sure they purchased culturally appropriate food that was easy for them to prepare. The Chore Service Program was eventually folded into the Home Aide Program.

Just as important, these CASL employees sat with seniors in their homes simply to engage in conversation. Most of these seniors had limited English-language skills and were living alone in Chinatown. Social interactions with CASL staff often provided the only face-to-face contact these seniors received during the week.

CASL's services were crucial to allowing seniors to live safely and happily in their homes. When the new building on 24th Place opened in 1985, CASL was providing services to more than one thousand seniors a year in Chinatown. Bernie, the CASL board, and staff still wanted to do more. Soon they would have reasons to expand thanks to a social worker out of Toronto.

| | |

Like the CASL founders, Larry So was born and raised in Hong Kong. He studied social work at the University of Hong Kong, and upon graduation in 1975, he found a job in community development at a Hong Kong YMCA. Larry spent the next decade and a half working as a social worker in Hong Kong at a time when the field was still developing there. In 1989, he moved to Toronto and signed a two-year contract for a social work job. But in 1991 when his contract was running out, Larry learned from a friend about a social service agency in Chicago's Chinatown. The attraction of working in a Chinese community with clients who spoke Cantonese was too much of a pull for Larry to stay in Toronto. He applied for the job at CASL.

Bernie hired him to oversee the youth programs, immigrant services, and to work with seniors at CASL. It wasn't easy for Larry to arrive in Chicago and suddenly be placed into a program director position for a community of people he didn't know. "I was grateful to Bernie for being my mentor and teaching me about the U.S. social work system," Larry explained. "Bernie showed me the ropes and was very supportive."

The space at 24th Place quickly filled up after CASL moved in half a decade earlier, so Larry mainly worked out of the youth center on Canal Street. And thanks to his extensive experience in Hong Kong and his two years in Toronto, he was able to help Bernie write proposals for youth and senior programs and to develop these programs when they received funding.

He also took notice of the seniors in Chinatown and, like Bernie and the other founders, knew what it felt like to immigrate and start anew. But the seniors CASL served—even those with physical mobility—remained confined to Chinatown, which hadn't changed since Eleanor So taught ESL fifteen years earlier. Wanting to help seniors lead a more fulfilling life rather than spending their days inside their homes, he came up with the idea of offering them an activity in the morning before his workday began. Tai chi seemed a natural choice because many of the seniors had exposure to it, whether practicing it themselves or observing it in parks.

Space at CASL continued to be a problem, so Larry held the tai chi classes in the youth center. "At first, ten to fifteen joined, but later it went up to thirty," Larry recalled. The seniors would all head home after the 7:30 a.m. class finished before Larry started work at 9:00 a.m. "I knew they wanted to do more, but CASL didn't have much else to offer them. I wanted to find ways to keep them engaged."

Since the class began so early, most of the seniors hadn't yet eaten breakfast when they arrived at CASL. Larry figured they would not only enjoy something to eat after their exercise, but a simple meal would also keep them engaged with CASL and would give them a stronger sense of community. "I talked to Bernie about providing something simple to eat and tea. She was supportive," Larry said. But there was no money in the budget even for morning refreshments. Every dollar was allocated to other programs, and even then, CASL's funds were stretched thin. Bernie apologized that she could not help but told Larry not to give up. There are always ways to find resources.

Larry decided to speak with CASL volunteers about ways to provide a simple breakfast and tea. Together, they came up with the idea of asking local bakeries if they could supply bread. Certainly, that would be easy to transport and would not be a huge loss for the bakeries. And sure enough, some bakeries agreed. The volunteers would pick up loaves of bread each morning and make tea so Larry could run the tai chi class as scheduled without having to worry about racing around Chinatown beforehand.

"The seniors enjoyed bread and tea and started talking about their day-to-day issues," Larry recalled. "This was the start of the senior center." As Larry listened to the seniors and heard of their wishes for more interaction, he reported these details back to Bernie so CASL could figure out ways to better help them. It would be very difficult to offer more senior programs at the youth center or the 24th Place building, the latter of which was also booked with the Chef Training Program, counseling space, and arts programming. To Larry and Bernie, it seemed pretty apparent that a dedicated senior center would be needed if they were to form a cohesive senior community.

| | | |

Larry also noticed something about the winters in Chicago. Although snow and icy conditions were not new to him after a couple of winters in Toronto, he found it challenging to engage with seniors in the winter. There was such a worry about seniors falling on the ice because it's not uncommon to break a hip with even a seemingly simple fall. And when seniors break a hip, more often than not it leads to more debilitating health issues from which they may never recover. So CASL warned its seniors against walking outside in the winter when there was ice on the ground. The seniors paid attention, but that meant Larry's tai chi classes slowed down during the winter months and the seniors were without any type of social outlet.

This problem started carrying over to the spring and summer months. "They didn't feel motivated to return after a long winter," Larry remembered. He wanted to come up with a solution to bring them back to CASL. If CASL didn't have the funds for a few loaves of bread each day, Larry knew it would not be able to help him with transportation needs. "It wasn't hard to start programs at CASL," he recalled, "but funding was always an issue. If there were needs in the community,

CASL would find money for programs. The different programs competed for funds, though." In the case of getting seniors safely to CASL, Larry could not wait for funding and once again turned to volunteers.

"I mobilized volunteers to use their cars and pick up seniors in the morning and take them to CASL," Larry said. Enough volunteers happily agreed, so the senior transportation issue was solved. It would later transform into a regular part of CASL, with dedicated vans complete with seat belts and comfortable seating as well as professional drivers. But back in the early 1990s, Larry So did what Bernie had been doing for over a decade: when there was a need, he found a solution. With a reliable form of transportation and a caring volunteer base to help seniors in and out of their cars to ensure safety, Chinatown seniors could once again participate in socialization programs with others their age.

| | |

In 1977, just before CASL was founded, the United States government passed Title XX of the Social Security Act, which included stipulations and funding for senior employment programs. Larry helped seniors interested in seeking employment and found ways to train them, whether it was working in restaurants or taking care of young children. "There were about fifty seniors in this program," Larry recalled.

He also helped seniors apply for a low-income gas subsidy program. Similar to the Circuit Breaker program that kicked off CASL's social services, this program also helped seniors with their gas bills. They would apply in September with the help of CASL staff and volunteers and receive a partial reimbursement check in October or November. As with all of these programs, Larry found the seniors to be very receptive and not too inhibited to refuse help. Unlike most of CASL's clients, some lived beyond the borders of Chinatown. "Not everyone was Chinese in this CASL program," Larry said. "They also came from Bridgeport and other parts of the greater community."

| | |

Larry's early work with the seniors, especially his tai chi classes, breakfast social gatherings, and transportation arrangements, showed Bernie and the CASL board that older adults could really benefit from more services and programs. By 1993, Larry had hired a tai chi master to teach the seniors. After class, the seniors would continue to stay back and talk about their wishes and started asking for more of a voice at CASL. These seniors started to think that they could do more but on their own.

In 1993, seventeen seniors came together to form the Pine Tree Senior Council to give them more opportunities to socialize, promote Chinese culture, and just be a support for one another as they all experienced similar issues when it comes to aging: declining health, loneliness, and a desire to keep active in their twilight years. They also felt it was important to have a group of seniors available to visit sick members at home. They would notice an absence if a member stopped showing up for a few days, so there was an accountability system. The Pine Tree Senior Council was completely self-run and advocated on behalf of Chinatown seniors, even those who were not involved with CASL.

The Pine Tree Senior Council exemplifies what CASL stands for—namely that they are filling a need by providing services that weren't offered before they organized themselves. Funding is always an issue, and when the Pine Tree Senior Council started, members paid a $20 annual fee. They also received donations from local merchants. Over the years, they've been able to recruit dedicated volunteers to help out. And when a need seems greater than the resources available, some of the members who are more well-off than others chip in to make these programs happen.

Seniors also came together to sing Chinese and American songs. They would practice once a week to be ready to perform at CASL's social events and other celebrations organized by the Pine Tree Senior Council. Their singing group was completely self-sufficient and run by their own members.

The seniors put together a publishing committee that started a newsletter in July 1993 to explain the name of their new council: Pine trees are evergreens and are always lively. They never fade, even in the winter. This first newsletter also included information about CASL that pertained to seniors, including calligraphy classes, drop-in center activities, cultural discussions, and medical information. They also reported on news from the American Association of Retired Persons (now known as the AARP). Way back before the internet, it was difficult for Chinatown seniors to otherwise learn about this information, especially in publications printed in Chinese. The publishing committee printed one thousand copies to distribute around Chinatown, and Pine Tree members put in their own money to print the newsletter. They also solicited local merchants for donations.

Soon after it was founded, the Pine Tree Senior Council started celebrating its members' birthdays on a quarterly basis and has continued to this day. About a dozen years after its founding, the Pine Tree Senior Council started giving away red envelopes with money inside to celebrants on their eightieth birthdays, a lucky number in Chinese culture. Also in Chinese culture, red envelopes are the traditional means of giving monetary gifts at the Lunar New Year, weddings, babies' first-month parties, and other milestone celebrations. Again, members and local business owners chipped in to donate funds for these gifts. The Pine Tree singing group would perform at these birthday parties. The seniors felt that it was important to celebrate a milestone birthday, especially when many of them lived alone or only with a spouse. The seniors also felt that it was important to gather around positive occasions like birthdays.

Lunar New Year and Christmas were other holidays that called for gatherings and celebrations. They viewed Christmas as an American holiday and felt proud to participate in this winter tradition. Lunar New Year is the most prominent holiday in Chinese culture, so it was also important for the seniors to be able to celebrate it, even though few outside Asian communities at that time knew about it.

The Pine Tree Senior Council also worked with travel agencies to arrange trips not just outside Chicago but sometimes outside of the United States. Each year, they would offer one trip; some trips included three days in Toronto, seven days in San Francisco, five days in Seattle, seven days in Las Vegas, five days in New York, four days in Tennessee, three days in Wisconsin, and seven days at Yellowstone. Local travel agencies would give the group special senior rates, and all participants would pay their own fees. Taking ownership of these trips meant a lot to the seniors and they especially appreciated the time to themselves, socializing with others their age who could speak a common language and could understand their day-to-day lives in Chicago. When their children take them on vacation, the seniors are always expected to watch their grandchildren both during the day and in the evenings, so they rarely have time to themselves. They loved their families—there was no doubt of that—but vacations are meant to be relaxing and time taken for oneself. That was rarely the case on family vacations, but these senior trips were a different story.

The trips were usually taken by bus, and CASL would send a staff member or two just to make sure things ran smoothly and safely and to interpret for the seniors if the need arose. Most trips would usually attract more than sixty seniors, filling up two coach buses.

As the years went by, Pine Tree added more classes. In 2006, they started both a calligraphy and a painting class, each held twice a week. These classes began with only five to six seniors, but now more than forty people participate. Some of the seniors have worked as professional calligraphers and have exhibited their work in shows organized by the Pine Tree Senior Council. When the city of Chicago was bidding to host the 2016 Olympics, a number of Pine Tree members created calligraphy scrolls to promote Chicago as an Olympic host. These scrolls were exhibited at the State of Illinois Building during the bidding period.

CASL has been proud to include the Pine Tree Senior Council under its umbrella because it is their only program that supports the independence of the senior community. The council has hired a staff member—funded by the U.S. Health and Human Services' Title V program—to take care of administrative matters. In 1994, then—Illinois governor Jim Edgar recognized the Pine Tree Senior Council with the Governor's Town Award.

As of this writing, the Pine Tree Senior Council is still going strong. For an annual fee of $26, seniors still enjoy quarterly birthday banquets at a local Chinese restaurant, occupying forty tables of ten people each. Even with an attendance of four hundred people, the eight-to-ten-course banquet is attended on a first-come, first-served basis. Normally, participants each chip in $10 for the banquet, but they have not had to pay for a number of years thanks to the generosity of anonymous donors.

| | |

After Larry's tai chi class grew in size and popularity, it became apparent that seniors would need a meeting place of their own. In 1994, a small house next to the main building on 24th Place became available. CASL bought this property and opened a dedicated senior center at 306 West 24th Place, a cozy space of one thousand square feet that allowed CASL to formalize its senior programs. "It provided a space for community senior groups and operated a drop-in center," Larry recalled. The Elderly Services Department was born and would also include a classroom, counseling space, and craft corner.

Two full-time nurses were hired for this new senior center. In 1994 alone, the Elderly Services Department served sixty-nine seniors. Four years later, that number would more than double.

The CASL founders realized early on the importance of engaging seniors. Arts and crafts classes are a good way to keep seniors active and to provide them with opportunities to socialize with others who speak the same language. Photo courtesy of the Chinese American Service League.

When the former truck garage could not accommodate all of the needs of the senior community, CASL opened one of three additional buildings for senior activities. This house at 306 West 24th Place included a small front garden for seniors to grow vegetables and flowers. Photo courtesy of the Chinese American Service League.

CASL would soon expand even more on 24th Place, as it was able to occupy two more buildings on that street: an Elderly Services Center at 300 West 24th Place and an annex to use for meetings and offices at 304 West 24th Place. Apart from the youth center on Canal Street, CASL's programs were now all centered on 24th Place.

For the time being, acquiring more buildings seemed to be the best solution to providing more space and services to Chinatown residents, but it was truly just a short-term solution. Maintenance needs differed among the different buildings, and after a decade, the former truck garage needed more renovations to keep the structure from falling apart. The half-mile walk from the cluster of buildings on 24th Place to the youth center on Canal Street would add up if staff had to travel from one area to the other and were already pressed for time. Bernie kept her eyes open for a larger space, but there just didn't seem to be a central building that could accommodate all of CASL's clients and programs under one roof.

| | | |

In speaking with seniors, especially those in the Pine Tree Senior Council, Larry saw another need for the community. Seniors didn't have a place where they could all live together. There was a senior living apartment in Chinatown, but it wasn't a Chinese building per se and the residents came from a variety of backgrounds. Living among a diverse population provides for rich experiences, but it can be difficult for older Chicago residents without English-language skills who don't have anyone around to interpret.

Larry wondered if CASL could build senior apartments that would allow for easy interaction among neighbors and could even include a communal area where residents could gather for social programs without leaving the building. Bernie was immediately interested. Land, of course, was an issue. "There was a piece of land near the railway yard," Larry said, "but it was polluted, so they gave up that idea."

In the three short years since Larry started at CASL, his early morning tai chi class had developed into a dedicated senior center to provide a nurturing community for the elderly in Chinatown. Yet for all of his great work with CASL, his tenure there would end in 1994 when his mother required more care. He had been away from Hong Kong for fifteen years at that point and decided it was time to return to help her. Once back in Hong Kong, he was able to continue to work as a social worker and retired early in 2002. But retirement would not last for long when he took a part-time job teaching social work at the Macao Polytechnic University, or Universidade Politecnica de Macau as it's known in Portuguese. With his rich experience in Hong Kong, Toronto, and at CASL, Larry So helped build the program—the only one of its kind in Macau—and ended up teaching there full time until he finally retired in 2014 at the age of sixty-five.

Larry's story is remarkable, but it's not atypical of people who have worked at CASL. When he saw needs among Chinatown seniors, he was able to put those needs into action thanks to support from Bernie and the CASL board. This was, after all, CASL's own approach to getting things done. Bernie's roll-up-your-sleeves approach to problem-solving and work ethic are common among immigrants from all over the world who make Chicago their home.

|||||||||||||||||||||||||||||||||||||||||||||||||||||||||||||||||||||||||||||||||||||||||||||||||||||||||||||||||||||||||||||

Canto-Pop Comes to CASL

In 1994, Canto-Pop had become more popular than ever in Hong Kong and in Cantonese-speaking communities around the world as pop performers Jacky Cheung, Leon Lai, Aaron Kwok, and Andy Lau wowed fans as the "Four Heavenly Kings."

So it was quite a feat when CASL arranged for Jacky Cheung and Sandy Lam, a Canto-pop "diva" to headline—pro bono—a benefit in Chicago to raise money for a $2 million capital campaign to renovate

CASL's 24th Place building as well as the different senior buildings. CASL also needed more funds for its ever-growing programs and services.

Sandy Lam is known for her 1987 Cantonese rendition of Berlin's "Take My Breath Away," which was featured in Wong Kar Wai's 1988 film *As Tears Go By*. Lam was drawn to the benefit because she was committed to charity work, especially when it involved children. Jacky Cheung was also a respected actor during the golden era of Hong Kong's film industry in the 1980s and '90s and felt particularly close to CASL's mission of giving back to Chinese communities.

CASL even involved teens at the youth center and held a contest to design a concert poster that could be used to advertise the event. A fifteen-year-old student named Lisa Lee created a black-and-red poster with both Chinese and English writing to promote the concert.

The concert was held at the Arie Crown Theater in Chicago's McCormick Place convention center in October 1994. As the *Chicago Tribune* reported, the concert was "a capacity, largely college-age, crowd."[1] Linda Yu and Chicago's WGN Channel 9's Joanie Lum introduced the stars and

Fifteen-year-old Youth Center participant Lisa Lee designed this poster to promote CASL's 1994 Canto-pop benefit concert in Chicago. Photo courtesy of the Chinese American Service League.

NBC Channel 5's Nesita Kwan served as emcee, speaking in Cantonese and English. Lum and Kwan were part of Linda Yu's CASL advisory board. The concert raised close to $100,000 for the capital campaign, and even though it may not have reached the intended goal, it was still a successful evening that brought together young people and much needed funds for CASL.

The energy it took to produce this concert, often working with the artists in a time zone fourteen hours ahead of Chicago, was grueling and involved overnight phone calls to arrange the logistics of their travels and itinerary in Chicago. The work did not stop once the singers arrived for the concert and the euphoria from the concert did not die down until Bernie and Monica Tang saw the singers off at O'Hare. As they turned to leave the airport, both women literally collapsed at the end of the moving walkway. Bernie turned to Monica, picked her up, and said, "It's okay that we failed and didn't raise what we need. Let's stand up and try something else. Tomorrow will be a better day."

The Canto-pop concert was the first and last CASL arranged.

14

Senior Housing Becomes a Reality

Larry So's vision of providing Chinatown seniors with affordable housing struck a chord with Bernie and the CASL board and lingered after he had returned to Hong Kong to care for his mother. As growing numbers of seniors turned to CASL for socialization and camaraderie, the agency knew it was time to start putting a plan into action to bring its own senior housing to Chinatown. With a dedicated building for Chinatown seniors, CASL could more easily provide in-home services as well as socialization programs in common areas that would be open to all residents.

In 1994, CASL applied for a grant from the U.S. Department of Housing and Urban Development, or HUD as it's more commonly referred. In the application, CASL explained that helping the elderly had always been a core part of the agency and that housing would provide the community with new and important socialization capabilities. When seniors are happy and lead fulfilling lives, they tend to have fewer health issues and go on to live longer.

But it was highly unusual for a first-time applicant to receive funding from a HUD grant. Bernie was not deterred and felt it wouldn't hurt to try. Even if the application were denied, there was still value in applying in hopes there could always be a next time and that one of those times would be successful.

CASL learned of the availability of a parcel of land that had been part of the old railroad yards, the same land that had been proposed when Larry first brought up the idea of senior housing. Since those initial talks, Ping Tom had helped restore that land and the specific plot of land CASL was eyeing was conveniently located on the corner of Princeton Avenue and Tan Court, a short walking distance to the new Chinatown Square that Ping Tom also helped develop. Restaurants and

Mayor Richard M. Daley speaks at the senior housing ground breaking. Seated on the far left is the developer, Ray Chin. Photo courtesy of the Chinese American Service League.

cafés like Saint Anna Bakery were in Chinatown Square, as were Chinese grocery stores, doctors and dentists, barbers and salons, and traditional Chinese medicine pharmacies.

A local builder named Ray Chin was brought on to draw up plans for the new housing complex, modeling it after government apartments in Hong Kong. If CASL could secure a HUD grant, its new senior housing would literally be a stone's throw from many of the shops and services the seniors would need to access on a daily basis.

No one at CASL, neither Bernie nor the board members, paid much attention to the time that lapsed between submitting the grant application and the time in which one would expect to hear an answer. It just wasn't on their radars because they were so sure their proposal would not be successful in this first attempt. HUD had other ideas.

When notice of their successful application came through, every staff member at CASL felt part of a larger mission. CASL would no longer only work out of older, run-down buildings in Chinatown. It would finally have the opportunity to construct its own residential building from the ground up, according to the needs of the seniors it would serve. HUD awarded CASL a grant of $6.7 million to build a ninety-one-unit facility.

Before Bernie and the CASL board could start thinking about construction, they consulted a feng shui expert to make sure the position of the building balanced with the elements of nature in the surrounding area. Going back thousands of years, feng shui is also known as Chinese geomancy and translates to "wind and water." It takes into account properties of nature like bodies of water and mountains and qi, or cosmic energy.

In the CASL founders' home city of Hong Kong, feng shui is serious business in the construction industry. It is the reason there's a gaping "hole" in a residential building in swank Repulse Bay and why I. M. Pei, one of the most celebrated architects in modern history, amended his design for Hong Kong's Bank of China Tower after feng shui masters declared the X motifs and sharp edges antithetical to the bank's purpose, which is to make and safeguard money.

CASL is a nonprofit organization, so finances didn't factor into the design, but health, longevity, and happiness were central to its mission. Most important of all, seniors in the community told the CASL board that many would feel wary about moving to the new building if a feng shui expert were not brought on to this project.

The feng shui master picked the colors for the exterior and interior, which included a partial brick exterior and other surfaces painted in light blue and a terra-cotta color. The shape of the building resembled a fish, which in Chinese culture represents an abundance of wealth and food, more than what one could hope for. But it was Bernie's husband, Albert, who proposed the name for the building. Visible from a block away, bold red Chinese characters of 樂宜居, which in English means "happy to live here," appear on the side of the building. Large lettering is a popular exterior style for government-funded apartment buildings in Hong Kong to bring good fortune to the people residing there, and even this small detail showed the seniors that this new building would be a welcoming and nurturing home for them. Two decades after the senior housing opened, it would be named the Albert and Bernie Wong Senior Living Community.

When spaces opened up before the construction was completed, the response was so great that a line formed at CASL's central office on 24th Place at six o'clock the night before the application process started. More than three hundred people showed up for ninety-one units. As of 2022, the waiting list for CASL's senior housing has been a decade.

To celebrate the opening of the building in September 1998, Mayor Richard M. Daley gave the keynote speech. A lion dance—consisting of two children from the youth program under a colorful costume of blue, red, orange, green, and pink

CASL's senior housing building, designed with input from a feng shui master and modeled after apartment buildings in Hong Kong. The Chinese characters can be translated as "happy to live here." Photo courtesy of Jacinta Wong.

cloth scales—ushered in a prosperous beginning. The dancer at the front of the costume held a giant lion's head, moving it up and down to the accompaniment of a drum, while the other dancer lifted the tail end. Lion dances traditionally inaugurate new businesses in Chinatown as well as Lunar New Year events.

The residents came together to form a tenant council with elected officers and floor leaders. CASL supports the residents by providing a full-time social worker on the premises to ensure the seniors' needs are being addressed.

A year before the senior building opened, CASL started an associate board to engage young professionals in Chicago—mainly in their twenties and thirties, including Bernie's daughter, Jacinta—to take on fundraising and service project roles at CASL, much like Linda Yu's advisory board. Each Thanksgiving, the associate board puts together baskets of food for the residents of the senior building and to other seniors in Chinatown.

This new addition gave Bernie and the board the idea that they could also use a new, centralized building that could house programs and administration all under one roof. The four buildings on 24th Place could barely contain the clients who visited CASL on a daily basis and the youth center suffered from weather-related repairs and wasn't feasible as a long-term option. Even with the big Canto-pop fundraiser in 1994, there wasn't enough money to take care of building mainte-nance. It was starting to seem imprudent to continue to throw money—money that was not easy to come by in the first place—into these buildings when they just weren't in good enough shape to meet the growing needs of Chinatown residents.

It was time to look for a new home and one that could be tailored to CASL's every need.

15

CASL Needs a New Home

Compared to other Chinatowns around the country and in Canada, one of the unusual features of Chicago's is that it is neither landlocked nor overbuilt. On top of that, the Chinese community in Chicago has continued to grow into communities adjacent to the core of Chinatown. Chicago's Chinatown also hasn't become gentrified. At the end of the 1990s, some of the same railroad yard that Ping Tom and others developed to use for Chinatown residents—both residential and commercial space—was still vacant and available for construction. There was even a space across the street from the senior housing building on Tan Court and Princeton Avenue that was owned by the Chicago Board of Education.

Bernie and the CASL board wanted that plot of land for a central building because it was in such close proximity to the senior housing building. But as with all of CASL's past expansions, this one would need money on a scale they had never dealt with before and a way to purchase the land.

Since the land wasn't being used, Bernie and the board asked about purchasing it for a new CASL building. Chicago Public Schools CEO Paul Vallas and Chicago School Board president Gery Chico agreed and worked with CASL to facilitate their purchase of this land. CASL also appealed to the Washington Square Health Foundation for a loan for this new building. And in 1999, CASL launched a new capital campaign, the largest in its then-twenty-year history, with a goal of raising $9.2 million to cover the construction costs, architectural design, furnishings, and staff salaries during this time.

Linda Yu was naturally the honorary chair of the capital campaign. Joining her was Maggie Daley, wife of Mayor Richard M. Daley. It was no small feat to raise this much money. CASL tapped into old supporters like the Chicago Community

Trust, which had been there from the beginning. The Kresge Foundation provided a matching grant, as it had done in the past. Bernard Lee, a longtime supporter and friend of CASL, donated $300,000, which at that time was the largest individual gift the agency had ever received. When others in the community saw that Lee had given that much, they became inspired to contribute, too. More than eight hundred local businesses donated almost $100,000 during a Chinese-language radiothon in the spring of 2003. CASL staff gave more than $30,000 in individual donations. There is no greater testament to a workplace than when staff members contribute to their employer, especially when they often didn't have extra money to spare.

These donations got CASL off to a great start, but there was so much more work to be done and it soon became apparent that Bernie would have to devote all of her time to the campaign. By 2000, CASL employed two hundred paid staff members and served more than fifteen thousand clients a year. Bernie had remained the constant force behind CASL all these years—with the full support of longtime board member and cofounder Esther Wong—but her work in developing programming, fundraising, and connecting with politicians and business leaders was proving too much even for her.

The CASL board decided to add an executive director position and change Bernie's role into that of CASL's president, similar to a CEO. In her new role, Bernie could continue to oversee the agency but concentrate her efforts on fundraising for the new building, as well as to remain the face of CASL when it came to public relations and community engagement.

Esther had also been a constant at CASL since the beginning, serving on the board for all those years and overseeing the program committee. She volunteered countless hours with CASL, including interpreting for Elaine Wong when she provided pro bono child psychology consultations for fifteen years. C. W. and Heidi Chan were the only other original founders who had stayed on after the others moved away in the early 1980s. At the end of that decade, they, too, had stepped off the board. Although C. W. remained a vital leader in Chinatown through his work with the Coalition for a Better Chinese American Community, by 2000 Esther was the only remaining founder on the CASL board.

Esther was the perfect person to step into this new executive director position. She had a rich social work background from when she was employed at the Chicago Child Care Society—one of the oldest social service agencies in Illinois—to work with teen parents. She also worked for the Chicago Board of Health before managing a couple of family businesses, including serving as bookkeeper for a wholesale seafood business her husband David and C. W. opened in Chicago.

After they sold this business in 2001, Esther went on to work as a staff consultant at CASL in 2001 and the following year became the agency's executive director.

Bernie and Esther were not related, but both had the same surname. "Sometimes people called me 'Bernie Wong' and that was an honor," Esther recalled. "Others thought we were sisters and addressed letters to Bernie and Esther Wong." The two old friends and cofounders would bring CASL into the new millennium and would work side by side until Bernie's retirement in 2016 and Esther's the following year.

| | |

Chicago developer Ray Chin, who had completed the senior apartment building, continued to advise CASL pro bono. When it came time to look for an architect for CASL's new building, Chin thought it would be a good idea to seek out bids from a range of firms regardless of their background in Chinese culture.[1] He hoped CASL would find the best possible fit for its new home. His firm, R. M. Chin and Associates, went on to oversee the entirety of the construction and assisted the CASL management with questions that arose.

CASL received bids from seven architectural firms with designs that served the utilitarian and cultural needs of Chinatown residents.[2] Six of the architects came up with concepts that appeared inviting and uniquely blended with the environment of the area, complementing the commercial and residential architecture and natural surroundings—namely, the trees and shrubbery in the very western part of Ping Tom Park and a stretch of shoreline along the south branch of the Chicago River directly opposite CASL's new building site. But the problem with these designs was that some included areas like large stairwells and courtyards that could not be used for programs and office space.

The seventh design, from an up-and-coming architect named Jeanne Gang, had a different idea. Gang was born and raised in Illinois and had opened her own architectural firm in 1997 after a stint working in Rotterdam under the guidance of renowned Dutch architect Rem Koolhaas.

Jeanne Gang was less experienced than the more established architects who had submitted bids, but Bernie and the CASL board weren't just impressed with Jeanne's designs; they also appreciated the attention and time she could devote to this project. Few in the early planning meetings for the new building could have envisioned just how high Gang's star would rise, not just in Chicago but around the world. In 2019, Gang's firm was selected to oversee the $8.5 billion redesign and expansion of O'Hare airport's international terminal.

Architect Jeanne Gang presenting her concept for a new CASL building to CASL's board of directors. Gang had just started her own firm a couple years earlier and would go on to become not only one of Chicago's leading architects but renowned around the world. Photo courtesy of the Chinese American Service League.

Talks began in 1998, and through communication with Bernie and the CASL board, Gang knew that this building needed to go beyond the typical, nondescript design of nonprofit agencies. It would incorporate space for all of its programs and offices for staff. There was a need for a grand hall to hold performances, large-scale meetings, and gatherings for festivals and other special events. Because CASL used kitchens for different uses, staff hoped the new building could include separate kitchen space for the culinary program and for food preparation. The building would also require dedicated space for the Early Childhood Education Center and the Adult Day Service.

The CASL board and Bernie originally envisioned this new building as a two-story structure, but somewhere during the planning stages, it soon become obvious that two floors would not be enough to hold all of the programs—all of which were growing—as well as classrooms, offices, and a community hall. The Employment and Training Program would add a youth component, which would need more space. CASL also planned a new Community Technology Center to teach clients computer skills and ways to become internet savvy in order to stay competitive in the job market. The Child Development Center had become accredited by the

National Association for the Education of Young Children; the additional space meant CASL could hire more teacher specialists for its programs. The building also would allow breast cancer screenings—inspired by Bernie's own fight with breast cancer in the late 1980s—and a program to help families apply for KidsCare insurance.

By the time the overall design was approved, the usable space had been expanded from its original twenty thousand square feet on two floors to thirty-six thousand square feet over three floors.

Gang wrote about her inspiration for the new building. "Chinatown's context consists of commercial buildings with exuberantly applied Chinese ornament such as pagoda roofs, as well as bare bones industrial buildings and a mix of old and newly constructed low-rise housing."[3]

The completed building was a rectangular concrete base with upper floors highlighted by titanium diamond-shaped cladding that both paid tribute to Chinese culture and would safeguard the building from the harsh Chicago winter weather. Celebrated *Chicago Tribune* architecture critic Blair Kamin wrote of the building, "It also puts a bracingly fresh spin on Chinese architecture. No sloping pagoda roofs. No banal brick facades tarted up in the symbolic Chinese colors of red and green. The Liu Building is an elegant silver box, the first in Chicago to be clad in the magical material of titanium. It would be considered a bright addition to the cityscape even if it weren't a community center that cost a modest $150 a square foot. Yet it is all the more impressive because that was the budget."[4]

The titanium siding was donated by longtime CASL board president Arthur Wong, a businessman who was born and raised in Chicago's Chinatown and owned, among others, a company that manufactured titanium. The siding seemed especially pronounced when the sun reflected against the tiles. The siding also suited the neighborhood, complementing the metal from the Orange Line "L" train that ran on a track across the street from CASL. The building fit nicely with the gargantuan steel lift bridges along the Chicago River that are visible from CASL's front entrance on Tan Court and even around the corner on Princeton Avenue.

Jeanne Gang explained why titanium was so suitable for this building: "Because of the inherent strength of titanium the architects were able to use the bent edge of the shingle itself to attach to the back-up layer instead of needing a secondary system of clips. The shingles were installed in an overlapping pattern to shed moisture. The two finishes of titanium cause interplay of light and color across the facades of the building creating a 'dragon skin' effect."[5]

The building's style also resonated with Chicago on a larger scale. As Blair Kamin explained, "On the one hand, it is a refreshing return to the old Chicago idea of the 'dumb box,' which saves money by virtue of its simple geometry and achieves aesthetic pop through one or two big moves and carefully worked-out details. On the other hand, it freshens that tradition, as well as Chinese architecture, with flourishes such as its wonderfully taut skin of titanium shingles, which are meant to evoke a dragon's scales."[6]

Gang sought input from all of CASL's program directors while she was developing plans for the interior parts of the building. And with three floors, there would be space for a two-story grand hall—which has since been named for Esther—with windows highlighted by vertical latticework reminiscent of traditional Chinese homes. An enclosed balcony with outdoor seating would be placed alongside the window of the grand hall. There would also be a full kitchen for the Chef Training Program as well as classrooms on the second floor. The third floor would be devoted to staff offices, while the first floor was planned to give equal space to the Childhood Development Center and Adult Day Service for senior citizens.

| | |

Brenda Arksey had been the director of CASL's Childhood Development Center for almost fifteen years when CASL started working with Jeanne Gang. "I asked for more program space and less storage space," Brenda recalled, "although we would soon need more storage space for toys, art supplies, and motor equipment. I also wanted space to hang the children's work, but the newly designed classrooms had one wall of windows and one with a bubble window and door, which left only two walls for pictures."

The wall with windows faced south to allow light in from both the east and the west and that looked out onto the playground directly accessible from the Early Childhood Center. "The playground is right off the classroom and the children could go out as much as possible, even in the winter. When the weather was too cold, the programs could book thirty minutes in the second-floor multipurpose room for large motor skills," Brenda said.

As for the classrooms' front walls with the entry doors, Gang designed these with rounded glass walls that looked out onto the hall. Brenda asked that the rounded walls be replaced with flat walls so there would be more wall space inside the room. Gang insisted the rounded walls were nonnegotiable. "It turned out to be wise because kids could sit on the bench along the rounded walls and look out the window to see their parents or caregivers," Brenda said. "It helped with transitions." They wouldn't feel so trapped and could still feel connected to their parents in the hallway, talking to other teachers. At the end of the day, the children who missed their parents or grandparents could sit on the bench and look out through the bubble to see them approaching. This allowed the children to feel more comfortable at the preschool until they fully adjusted.

Gang used other round interior design details to take away some of the bluntness of the building's straight edges. "The boxy design of the building caused Gang to create more round spaces indoors," Brenda said, "and, for example, the cubbies were arranged in a curve, which made it hard to store some things since there weren't straight edges, but we made do."

On the other side of the building, the Adult Day Service would occupy a secured wing so seniors of different cognitive abilities would not be able to wander away. The Adult Day Service wing would also have its own kitchen to prepare culturally appropriate meals for the seniors at breakfast and lunch, along with an afternoon snack. The seniors could occupy different rooms according to their language abilities. Cantonese and Toisanese speakers would meet in a larger meeting room that looked out to a small garden. There would be a smaller room next to that for Mandarin speakers and yet another room at the end of that hall for dance rehearsals, afternoon mah-jongg, and other activities that required more space like intergenerational gatherings.

The new building's interior design would need to be practical yet appealing to the wide range of CASL clients. Per the style of the new millennium, the ductwork was exposed inside the new building, but plenty of light could flow through the corridors and in the individual rooms with floor-to-ceiling windows. Four different shades of green—representing jade and echoing the feng shui principles of happiness and prosperity—would be used throughout the center, each color in a different part of the building. The original intentions of the design seem to have been lost over the years and these walls have since been painted over with a utilitarian off-white color.

Linoleum tiling would allow easy transportation within the building for strollers, wheelchairs, and walkers. In the multipurpose room, giant light fixtures resembling half doughnuts were taken from truck tire innertube molds. These larger fixtures intermingled with smaller white globe lights. Perhaps a coincidence, the truck tires paid homage to the 24th Place origins as a truck garage.

The first-floor lobby waiting area also used the same globe light fixtures. Originally, red couches and chairs were placed in the lobby for clients while they waited for an appointment. The color red is auspicious in Chinese culture and is a sign of good fortune and happiness. In later years, with a growing need to provide shelter to community members without a place to go during the day, these red couches and chairs were replaced by single-occupancy chairs to allow for more people.

Bernie had never felt more passionate about a CASL building than she was when she saw Studio Gang's design. As she stated at the time, "Studio Gang is more creative, slightly out of the ordinary, and we wanted a building that stands out. There are enough buildings that look like each other in Chinatown."[7]

Just as it had done with the senior housing building, CASL consulted a feng shui master to make sure all of the building's components provided balance, harmony, and alignment with the physical elements of CASL's surroundings. Because CASL faced part of the Chicago River and Ping Tom Park, the building would need to align with the properties of trees and water. And with the large, metal bridges on that branch of the river, visible on the street in front of CASL, the feng shui master would need to consider elements of metal, too.

The feng shui master would also review door and window placement throughout the building. An entrance could make or break a business or agency's success. But when he studied the blueprints, the feng shui master saw that the proposed entrance and a couple of trees would interfere with the building's qi. So the entrance was moved and the trees were cut down. Thankfully, this all happened well before construction began.

The new entrance of the current building looks out onto an open space that is part of Ping Tom Park. Natural light from this direction flows into the multipurpose room, but its windows included a steel lattice sunshade to protect the occupants from feeling too hot. The sunshade was designed to resemble bamboo, also approved by the feng shui master. A few other interior changes took place, too, including moving the location of Bernie's office and dropping the ceiling in that room.

The feng shui master passed away before construction commenced in January 2003, so a new adviser was brought in and only found issue with the placement of some electrical outlets.

| | |

Raising millions of dollars to fund this building was not easy. Although CASL had met its fundraising needs in the past, that all seemed like peanuts when compared to the cost of a brand-new building with a goal of $9.2 million.[8] The largest individual gifts had been in the six figures until a local realtor named Kam L. Liu stepped up.

Liu's story is similar to that of many of the CASL founders and the thousands of clients CASL has helped over the decades. Born in southern China, he emigrated to Hong Kong at the age of three and lived there with his adopted mother. Liu attended a Christian school in Hong Kong that used Mandarin as its instructional language. Although his native tongue is the Toisan dialect, he also learned Cantonese in Hong Kong. "I only had one year of English in Hong Kong," he said.

By the time he was in his early teens, his mother took him to Chicago so they could start a new life in the United States. It was 1963, two years before the historic Immigration and Nationality Act that would finally put an end to the Chinese Exclusion Act of 1882 and all the other restrictive laws that followed, grossly prohibiting immigration from Asian countries. Liu's mother was able to immigrate because her father was a U.S. citizen. At that time, her father was living in Chicago and working for Wayne Sit's upscale South Pacific Restaurant on Randolph Street, where diners were entertained with Polynesian dancers. Liu's arrival coincided with the time Bernie arrived in the United States to attend college in Iowa.

Liu and his mother lived on Chicago's northside, where he attended Waller High School, now Lincoln Park High School, yet he got to know Chinatown very well in his teens. "I worked on the weekends at a grocery story on the northwest corner of Cermak and Wentworth. I took the bus to Chinatown and worked four to five hours on Friday nights and thirteen hours on both Saturdays and Sundays. There's still a sign from the grocery store at the Chinatown museum," he recalled. After high school, he went on to study industrial engineering at University of Illinois at Chicago but had always had an interest in real estate. Although he continued to live on the northside as an adult, Liu saw an opportunity to bring more residents to Chinatown.

In the 1980s while most Chinatowns around the country saw stagnation or a decline in population and businesses, Chicago's Chinatown was a real estate developer's dream thanks in part to the reclaimed railroad yard, allowing Chinatown to expand north. But breaking into the real estate business there was not easy. Just as Bernie and the CASL founders had learned when they first organized social services, old traditions die slowly. "I was looked on as an outsider because I lived on the northside," Liu said.

As he started his real estate business, the custom in Chinatown was for unlicensed people to sell real estate without taking commissions. It was easy for these unlicensed brokers to find clients because buyers and sellers thought they were saving a lot by not having to pay a commissions—the bread and butter of any realtor's earnings.

Instead, these under-the-table realtors accepted red envelopes of money, up to the discretion of the buyer. Liu viewed his real estate career as a long-term way to give immigrants a chance to own their own homes. He felt he could only succeed if he studied for a realtor's license and ran his business above the ground.

Although homebuyers were accustomed to giving red envelopes to their realtors, somehow the concept of paying a regulated commission seemed scary and more costly. "It was hard to get business at first because people didn't want to pay the commission," Liu recalled. Business was slow going for Liu at first, but it picked up as buyers eventually realized it was best to work with a licensed realtor and one as passionate as Liu. For decades, he was the only licensed realtor in Chinatown who sold residential properties. "I never worked as an engineer and have been in real estate for forty-six years," he said in 2021.

Soon after CASL was founded, Liu married. He and his wife, Sadie, went on to have three sons, and while they continued to live on the northside, he always cherished his work in Chinatown. After CASL announced a new fundraising campaign for a new building, Liu pledged $1 million from his family. "If I couldn't raise the funds from my family, I would make up the difference," he said. His family's gift became the single largest donation to the building fund. Because of this generosity, the new CASL building was named for Kam L. Liu.

Before the building was completed, Liu and Sadie became regular participants in a ballroom dance group at the CASL youth center on Canal Street. Starting in 2004, the dance class moved to the second-floor Esther Wong Harmony Hall in the new building. When he made his donation, all he asked was for a floor in the grand hall that was large enough for ballroom dancing.

The ribbon-cutting ceremony at the opening of the Kam L. Liu Building on Tan Court. Local businesses provided flowers with messages of good fortune and prosperity, a traditional Chinese custom to celebrate a grand opening. Photo courtesy of the Chinese American Service League.

Liu, Sadie, and a regular group of fifty participants learned from a teacher from Taiwan every other Saturday. Participants would pay $10 a class, which would cover the teacher's salary and refreshments. The class went on hiatus for a year at the beginning of the pandemic but resumed after vaccines were available.

| | |

The Kam L. Liu Building was inaugurated the summer of 2004 with an outdoor ceremony attended by more than two hundred community leaders, local politicians, CASL clients and board members, and reporters from all of the major Chicago news stations. A podium stood outside, highlighted by a pink-and-red placard of the CASL logo just as Iris Ho and Paul Ho had designed twenty-five years earlier. A long strand of red firecrackers hung over the front door to be ignited to usher in good luck.

On either side of the podium stood two stone lions donated by the Chinese consulate in Chicago. No one was more relieved to see those lions in place before the building's entrance than Esther.

While the building was still in the planning stages, the Chinese consulate in Chicago generously offered to donate two stone lions to be placed in front of CASL's entrance. Sometimes called guardian lions or even foo dogs, these stone lions symbolize protection from harmful elements. The lions always come in a pair to bring balance or yin and yang. The male usually comes with a ball or globe under one front paw and a female with a cub under her paw.

During the building's planning phases, Bernie had traveled to China for a concert and spoke with the people in charge of sending the lions to CASL in Chicago. The lions would have to clear customs in the United States, but with the Chinese consulate involved, that would be no problem as it could explain why such large statues were arriving from China or the purpose they would serve.

But the lions ended up arriving during construction, well ahead of completion. Without a finished building, the lions could not be placed in their permanent positions in front of the CASL entrance. A storage facility was found and the pair would stay in this warehouse for months until it was time to put the final touches on the building and prepare for the grand opening.

It would have been much easier to bring the lions straight from customs to the CASL building. But now another delivery would need to be arranged to bring the lions from storage to Tan Court in Chinatown. Bernie was tied up with planning the opening day ceremony, including inviting guest speakers, other local politicians, and the local media. So Esther was put in charge of bringing the lions to CASL, which involved hiring a truck and movers that could lift such heavy statues. "Few people knew about all the logistics involved in getting the lions to

The two lions donated by the Consulate of the People's Republic of China. These lions, representing a male and a female, stand on either side of CASL's front doors to bring in good luck. Photo courtesy of the Chinese American Service League.

Chinatown," Esther recalled. But she got the job done and this challenge would symbolize her role as CASL's executive director. Bernie was the face of CASL, but Esther got things done in the background.

"We were both born in the year of the sheep, the attributes of which include gentleness, justice, sympathy, and thriftiness," Esther said years after the new building opened its doors. "But we had different Western zodiac signs, so that's where our personalities differed. We were confident we could reach our goals but had different paths in mind."

On the day of the inauguration ceremony, Tan Court was closed to traffic while dozens of colorful floral bouquets—draped with congratulatory messages printed on ribbons from local businesses—lined the curb in front of the new building. More than two hundred chairs were arranged on the street before the main entrance as the white stone lions stood proud with a sash of red ribbon tied around each. Bernie wove through the crowds, greeting her guests as if they were the only ones at the event. When the ceremony started, lion dancers performed before both the audience and their stone counterparts to usher in good fortune. A line of dignitaries held up a long ribbon and used that for the ribbon-cutting ceremony, including the CASL board president, Arthur Wong, who provided the titanium siding for the new building.

The corner of Tan Court and Princeton Avenue showcasing the different textures of CASL's Kam L. Liu Building. The small titanium squares resemble dragon scales and the metal latticework pays tribute to the window style in traditional Chinese homes. Photo courtesy of the Chinese American Service League.

C. W. and Esther were among other CASL founders who had returned for the opening ceremony. It must have seemed almost like a dream to think back twenty-five years when they first incorporated CASL and tried to help as many people in Chinatown as they had time and resources for. With 260 multilingual staff and more than 300 volunteers, CASL was able to touch the lives of 15,000 people each year when the new building opened in 2004.

The building would go on to receive a number of design awards during its first two years. In 2004, Studio Gang and the building were awarded the Distinguished Building Award Citation of Merit from the American Institute of Architects. It was also named "Project of the Year" in institutional construction by *Midwest Construction* magazine. In 2005, it won third place in the Richard H. Driehaus Foundation Awards Competition for Architectural Excellence in Community Design. That year, it also won the Best New Institutional Building design from the Friends of Downtown.

| | |

A later addition to the first-floor lobby has become the focal part of that space. The Zhou Brothers created *Passionate City*, a multipaneled artwork to serve as the agency's donor wall. It is made from sheets of painted metal that form a horizontal screen spanning the entire wall opposite the registration desk.

The different panels allow for donor names to be added all while providing a stunning art piece of yellow, purple, red, and other colors that complement the natural brightness of the room. Each panel represents the diversity of the community, but arranged all together, they show a single, united passionate city. This is the first part of the building new clients see, as well as anyone who walks into the front entrance. The Zhou Brothers have donated other pieces of art that are displayed throughout the building, all given in gratitude to their decades-long relationship with CASL.

PART IV

A New Home in the 2000s

16

Program Consolidation and Expansion

Ricky Lam, like many of the employees at CASL in the 1980s and 1990s, came to Chicago from Hong Kong and graduated in 1995 with a degree in human resources management from the University of Illinois at Chicago. "I learned about CASL after my wife's friend told me about it," he recalled, "About 70 percent of the staff was from Hong Kong then. Hong Kong immigrants knew what it was like to start over in a new place."

When Lam met with Bernie in 1995, she was impressed with his educational background. Human resources management would give Lam the foundation to work with clients of different backgrounds. Bernie offered him the job of Title V coordinator, and it didn't take Lam long to accept.

"The main goal of Title V was to help give seniors the confidence and self-esteem to live their best lives," Lam explained. "They came to the U.S. for a number of reasons, and Title V would give them more opportunities for work that went beyond kitchen jobs, which were often very tiring for seniors." Title V provided funding for seniors to find jobs that were suitable for their skills. For Chinatown residents, this was especially important because so many job openings involved restaurant work, which was easy to find but difficult to endure hours on end under stiflingly hot conditions.

As much as Lam enjoyed working with seniors and helping them find meaning in their new lives in Chicago, he saw an opportunity open in 2000 after he had been at CASL for five years. A manager position in his department became open and Lam felt it would provide him with more challenges. He applied and Bernie offered him the position. Lam would go on to head CASL's Employment and Training Department for the next seventeen years. This was just one example of the way Bernie invested in her staff, providing them with opportunities to rise up the ladder at CASL.

| | |

In 1999, CASL attracted another Hong Kong transplant named Ben Lau to its offices, based on its reputation for providing a wide range of services to Chinese immigrants. Coincidentally, Lau was there on his brother-in-law's behalf, not his own. "We knew CASL had employment counseling and my brother-in-law didn't know English," said Lau. "So we thought it would be a good place to receive counseling." Lau himself had been a teacher in Hong Kong and also the international news editor at *Tsing Tao Daily*, a prominent Hong Kong newspaper that started back in 1938. He never thought he would be the one to walk out of CASL that day with a new job and a new career.

At the time Lau walked into CASL to help his brother-in-law, there was one job developer in the Employment and Training Department that Ricky Lam managed. "He asked me if I would want to work at CASL as an employment counselor," Lau said. The job developer appreciated Lau's English skills, teaching background, and newspaper experience and felt that Ben would be a great fit for this open position. Lau started working for CASL on December 1, 1999 and would stay for the next two decades.

He worked for two years as an employment counselor before he was promoted to be an employment coordinator. By 2005, just after CASL moved to its new building on Tan Court, the agency received a grant from the city of Chicago to employ five more job counselors, a 500 percent increase in staffing in that department.

That same year, CASL was also awarded a grant from Charter One Bank, now U.S. Bank. Before the subprime mortgage crisis in 2008, a nearby Charter One branch employed a Chinese-speaking mortgage specialist who ended up spending most of her working hours accompanying Chinese clients to new homeowner workshops and serving as an interpreter. Interpreting wasn't part of her job description, nor was guiding people to workshops, but these clients didn't know anyone else who was familiar with financial terminology. It got to a point, however, that this mortgage specialist couldn't complete the work she was paid to do, so she went to her bosses to ask for help. Something had to change. Her bosses turned to CASL.

Charter One Bank felt that CASL could provide these same interpreting services, even in such a niche field, because it had Chinese-speaking staff and catered to Chinatown residents. Charter One's idea also included a grant to CASL to pay for staff to be trained in this terminology through HUD. Although Bernie and the board were usually adept at recognizing concerns in the community, this was a case in which another organization saw a need and turned to CASL for help.

By 2010, CASL's housing program was growing beyond anyone's expectations. Because Chicago's Chinatown was not considered to be gentrified, Chinese residents enjoy many more opportunities for homeownership than is the case in other Chinatowns around the country, where prices are out of reach for newly arrived immigrants.

To deal with the demand for more services, CASL decided to add a Housing and Financial Empowerment Department, which Lau managed. He and his colleagues advised clients on what to expect before and after purchasing a house or condo unit. "We provided education on renting homes, foreclosure, senior repairs, and energy assistance," Lau said. These services included both group classes and individual counseling.

Lau's department was federally accredited by HUD and he and his staff went through training to become HUD certified, including passing an examination. "CASL's department was the only bilingual Chinese housing department in Chicago approved by HUD. If a department doesn't have HUD approval, it cannot apply for federal grants," Lau said. Each housing counselor needs to be HUD certified as a requirement of employment or else cannot work in that position.

But there were other issues that seemed more rudimentary and that Lau had to develop from scratch. "My department received an employment grant from the mayor's office, which allowed me to develop a database program using Microsoft Access," Lau recalled. "At that time, the mayor's office didn't have its own job database, so each social service agency needed to have its own." Lau spoke about his database in Springfield, and later the mayor's office developed a centralized database modeled after Lau's.

In 2019, Lau felt like it was time to move on after a quarter century at CASL and left to become the executive director of the Chinese American Museum of Chicago. "The museum position gave me new challenges that I could tackle because of my training at CASL," said Lau, who as of the time of writing is no longer at the museum. "I learned the necessary skills to run the museum after twenty years of working under Bernie and Esther." In February 2023, the Asian American Coalition of Chicago presented Lau with the Exemplary Community Service Award in recognition of his outstanding leadership and dedicated service to the Chinese community.

The Chinese American Museum of Chicago

The Chinese American Museum of Chicago is located on 23rd Street in Chinatown and is not far from CASL's previous offices on Wentworth, Cermak, and 24th Place. The museum is a relatively new addition to Chicago's Chinatown but has quickly become one of its greatest treasures. Opened in 2005 in a former warehouse that was built in the late 1800s, the museum suffered a devastating fire in 2008 and had to close for renovations. Longtime CASL friend and former board member Raymond B. Lee and his wife, Jean, donated $1 million to fix the damaged areas and for improvements in other parts of the museum. Lee felt especially close to the museum because his family ran a wholesale food business in that building and Lee himself had slept on the building's third floor as a teen.

The museum's exhibits have rivaled its peer institutions in Chicago and includes permanent exhibits like "Great Wall to Great Lakes: Chinese Immigration to the Midwest," temporary ones like "The Chinese Helped Build the Railroad—The Railroad Helped Build America," film screenings, and an annual Lunar New Year celebration with music, lion dancing, calligraphy, and food.

17

Multigenerational Services in One Space

When Stacy Huang and her family immigrated to the United States from Toisan in southern China, everything about Chicago felt new and different. The Huangs moved from a subtropical town of just under a million along a coast of the Pearl River Delta to an inland city of three million with long winters and people who spoke a language different from theirs.

Stacy and her husband had two young daughters when they moved to Chicago in 2001. She found work right away in a Chinese restaurant but soon realized that waitressing was exhausting. "It was hard with two young daughters," Stacy said. Restaurant work left little time for her family. But a friendship with another waitress at that restaurant proved life-changing and would influence not only Stacy but also her husband, daughters, mother, and mother-in-law. The other waitress told her about CASL.

As it turned out, CASL at that time was looking for a receptionist to answer the phone and check in clients. The front desk usually had two or three receptionists so that no one, whether calling on the phone or arriving in person, would have to wait very long to be helped. It was a far cry from the days when Linda Yu found long lines of people waiting to see Bernie on the second-floor walk-up on Cermak.

Because Stacy was from Toisan, her language skills were exactly what CASL was looking for in a receptionist. "I can speak Toisanese, Cantonese, and Mandarin," Stacy said. With these three dialects or languages, Stacy would be able to communicate with most clients who came through CASL; she would also be able to practice English on a daily basis as she greeted visitors and clients who didn't speak Chinese.

When Stacy was hired as a receptionist, her elder daughter was three years old and enrolled in CASL's day care, just a stone's throw from the receptionists' desk. But her younger daughter was still just a baby and too young to attend any programs at CASL without a caregiver. Stacy could not quit her job to stay home with her daughter, but had no one else to care for her. She mentioned this to Bernie. Without pausing, Bernie told Stacy to bring her baby daughter to work. She could keep her secure behind the front desk, away from the traffic in and out of the building.

Working as a receptionist seemed much easier than waitressing on her feet all day, and Stacy enjoyed meeting different people as they came through CASL. Yet she worried at the beginning that she couldn't keep up and that her minimal English could interfere with her ability to do her job well. She spoke about this with Bernie and was quickly reassured. "Bernie told me to take it easy and not worry about training. She was confident I could learn the skills of a receptionist," Stacy said. There were certainly ample opportunities to practice English with visitors and clients who did not speak Chinese.

Stacy and her daughters weren't the only ones in her family to benefit from the community at CASL. Her husband also went to CASL to speak with a job counselor about the different opportunities available in Chicago, preferably outside Chinatown where his earning power would be greater and he could receive health benefits. Through CASL, he found a job at the Hilton Chicago, not too far from Chinatown on South Michigan Avenue. Once the largest hotel in the world, the Hilton Chicago started as the Stevens Hotel, developed by the father and grandfather of former Supreme Court justice John Paul Stevens, a Chicago native. During World War II, the hotel turned into military barracks after the U.S. Army bought the building. By the time of the Vietnam War protests at the 1968 Democratic National Convention, which took place in front of the hotel and were violently stopped by Mayor Richard J. Daley and the police, the hotel had been owned for two decades by Conrad Hilton. When Stacy's husband joined the banquet team at the Chicago Hilton decades later, he was part of a staff that prided itself as stewards of a Chicago institution and historic landmark.

Stacy and her husband were able to bring their mothers to Chicago, both of whom benefited from CASL's services. Stacy's mother attended English classes to help improve her communication skills in Chicago and to prepare for her citizenship exam, which she successfully passed. As of this writing, her mother lives in senior housing and moved in around 2008. Stacy's mother-in-law attended CASL's Adult Day Services for six to seven years, but after a fall resulting in a broken hip, she was no longer able to go out as much as before. "It was too scary for her to go out as much," Stacy said at the time of writing. "She can walk and speak just fine and is very sharp at ninety-eight." Stacy and her husband felt sad about this change in lifestyle but applied for her mother-in-law to receive home health care from CASL in the senior housing building, where she moved when she was in her early eighties.

Bernie was correct about Stacy's ability to learn her receptionist job well. After a while, answering the phone, greeting guests, and directing new clients all became second nature. Bernie saw that Stacy was great with people and could relate to them as recent immigrants, especially young families new to Chicago. Stacy was promoted to become an employment counselor and thrived in this position. "I put myself in my clients' shoes because I had been there at one point," she said.

As Stacy's daughters grew, they continued to call CASL their home, too. "My daughter Jenny attended the CASL after-school program as well as the summer jury duty program. She received a stipend, so was paid for the summer program. Both of my daughters went to Whitney Young High School," Stacy recalled.

When the family started learning about the college application process in the United States, Stacy began talking to other staff at CASL and one in the youth program couldn't say enough about small liberal arts colleges. "I had to look up the meaning of liberal arts in the dictionary," she said. Like many immigrants, Stacy and her husband had moved to the United States to give their children better opportunities than they had as children and adults. "At first, I worried a liberal arts education would not prepare my daughter for a practical job after graduation."

But as Stacy continued to talk to the CASL staff about her daughter's college applications, she started to realize that critical-thinking skills and a well-rounded education were actually things her family enjoyed the most about their new lives in Chicago. Her daughters certainly had a diverse group of classmates at Whitney Young, one of Chicago's most competitive public high schools, all while still hanging on to their Chinese roots through CASL programs and their parents' close connection to the agency. Stacy learned about scholarships her daughter could apply for, and before long, both of her daughters received full scholarships to study at Middlebury College in Vermont. "A liberal arts education was so important to my daughters and made their lives more meaningful," Stacy said. "I feel like people are comfortable around them because of their liberal arts education at Middlebury."

Stacy and her family were finally at a place where they had few worries. She had a satisfying job at CASL, her husband enjoyed his job at the Hilton, and their daughters did well in school. But without warning, her husband suffered a stroke from which he didn't fully recover and left him unable to work. "Fortunately, he had good insurance and could get proper medical care," Stacy said. Thanks to the union benefits from the Hilton, the family was saved from a great burden that often plagues Americans when they fall ill or become disabled. Even though the family was not financially destitute, Stacy worried about her husband being stuck at home all day while she was at work and their daughters were in school.

When people are unable to work and feel helpless, it's very easy to sink into depression. This was a big worry for Stacy. She was working under Esther at that time and expressed concerns about her husband's well-being. "Esther told me that my husband shouldn't be at home all day alone," Stacy said. As was typical of CASL and its founders, a solution was close at hand. Esther suggested that Stacy's husband participate in Pine Tree Senior Council to engage with others his age in a setting where he could communicate in his mother tongue. It didn't take long for him to follow Esther's advice. At the time of writing, he has been an active member of CASL's Pine Tree Senior Council and has found new meaning and friendships. "Since my husband was a banquet house staff at the Hilton," Stacy said, "he can contribute to the Pine Tree Senior Council, too."

When COVID-19 broke out, CASL had to make some staff changes as their services changed from in-person to remote. Stacy was devastated when she learned her job would be eliminated. She collected unemployment insurance for a year before finding a job as a receptionist at a senior housing apartment that is not affiliated with CASL. As sad as it was to leave CASL, Stacy is grateful for her time at the agency and the skills she learned for her new job. "My job in senior housing fits my passion to serve the community," she said. At the time of writing, she enjoyed helping seniors by interpreting between Chinese and English. She also helped seniors find more patience in their day-to-day lives.

Her current work is different from what she did at CASL because she works with only one age group now, but she is certain that her training and mentorship from Bernie and Esther not only prepared her well for this new job but also gave her a great life in Chicago. "Esther was always very friendly and interested in what my family was doing, including my daughters. She was so patient and a good listener. I'm very grateful to Esther. She said I never had to hide my family and that we were always welcomed at CASL."

Chinatown Library

CASL was not responsible for clearing out the former railroad yards or developing residential and commercial Chinatown over the last forty-five years. It did not start the Chinese American Museum of Chicago or build Ping Tom Park. But it does have connections to most of these initiatives, including another new addition in 2015.

For decades, the Chicago Public Library's Chinatown branch had occupied a small storefront space on Wentworth, south of the Chinatown gate. The space was tight but well used and well loved. With more residents moving into Chinatown after new housing went up in the old railroad yard area, the library could not accommodate the numbers of patrons that would visit at a given time.

Community organizer Rebecca Shi at the Coalition for a Better Chinese American Community made it her mission to bring the new library to Chinatown. The coalition is a dedicated advocacy organization founded by C. W. Chan after he stepped off the CASL board in the late 1980s. C. W. was appointed to serve on the library search committee to find an architect to design the new building. With more than a dozen initially interested, the committee narrowed the pool down to three architects, including Brian Lee at Skidmore, Owings & Merrill. Lee was also a CASL board member. "When Bernie learned I had just moved from San Francisco and was involved with the Chinatown Community Development Center board, she asked me to be on the CASL board," Lee said. With his team's vision of bringing Chinese elements to the new library building, their design won. The new contemporary building would epitomize what libraries mean to people today: a community center for everyone.

From the outside, the new Chinatown library building appears as an oval but is more of a triangle with rounded edges to fit the space where it stands on Archer and Wentworth Avenues, all in accordance with the principles of feng shui. The building also fits in well with the nearby Chinatown Red Line "L" station and train tracks.

Modeled after traditional Chinese hutongs, or courtyard homes, the library includes an open floor plan lined with a perimeter of windows. Natural light shines in through the ceiling, and the ground floor is visible from most spots on the second floor. The building also resembles the Bird's Nest stadium in Beijing that debuted at the 2008 Olympics. Both feature exterior steel beams, forming a nest. The Chinatown library's beams are vertical and reach beyond the top floor of the building, while the stadium in Beijing is made from curved beams.

According to the American Institute of Architects, "the Chicago Public Library, Chinatown Branch serves as a civic, educational, and social hub for the city's Chinatown neighborhood. The most visited branch in the Chicago Public Library system, the library provides a much-needed public gathering place geared toward community activities and technology-based learning. Anchored by a skylit two-story central atrium, the building's interiors are open concept, flexible, and sustainable, and feature daylighting, panoramic neighborhood views, with bright, comfortable furnishings for visitors of all ages, including a vibrant site-specific 60-foot mural on the history of Chicago's Chinatown painted by a local artist."[1]

The original design was to include a sign on the outside of the building with Chinese calligraphy of a proverb extolling bringing people together. That sign never materialized, but the building is still a focal point of the community and another example of a contemporary piece of architecture that brings in Chinese elements and serves the Chinatown community.

18

CASL's Impact and Recognition

Whereas senior staff like Ricky Lam, Ben Lau, and Monica Tang worked at CASL for decades under Bernie's guidance, not all young staff members would follow in their footsteps. Some CASL employees instead saw CASL as a stepping-stone to other opportunities outside Chinatown. CASL was quickly becoming the largest employer in Chinatown, even back in the 1990s, and to work in social services in the Chinese community for the most part meant working for CASL. A young Chicagoan named David Wu had other ideas. Growing up, Wu was involved with the Chinese Christian Union Church and got to know Chinatown when he did community service work there with his church. "My pastor asked college kids to live in Chinatown so they could better understand the needs there," Wu said. This philosophy was similar to that of the settlement house movement. "The church had been in the community for a long time but hadn't helped the community as much as I thought it could." The Chinese Christian Union Church was founded in 1915, shortly after Chicago's Chinatown uprooted to its current location.[1]

Wu's work with his church inspired him to study social work, and in 1989, he graduated with a master's in social work from the University of North Carolina at Chapel Hill. He returned home to Chicago and found a summer job at CASL right after graduation. "I coordinated a summer youth training program of twenty paid interns who were assigned to work with different staff around CASL," Wu said. As he worked out of the 24th Place former truck garage, he got to know Bernie, Esther, and C. W. that summer.

"I hadn't expected to work in Chinatown after finishing graduate school," Wu recalled. He left CASL after that summer and quickly found a permanent job in Uptown at the CMAA, the organization founded by Chinese Vietnamese refugees

Duc Huang and his daughter Yman Vien. Wu was hired as assistant director and served in that position for four years before he was promoted to executive director.

While at CMAA, Wu worked with Ed Silverman, founder of the Illinois Bureau of Refugee and Immigrant Services, and also learned about community building from him. "He thought it was best to build capacity in ethnic communities when it came to refugee resettlement. It was a unique strategy at the time," Wu remembered. Wu would serve as executive director of CMAA for a year before Chinatown called him back.

| | | |

In 1988, the On Leong Chinese Merchants Association Building on Wentworth and Cermak was confiscated by the federal government after an FBI bust for illegal activity in the building. The only historical building in Chinatown, it was constructed in the mid-1920s and is a masterpiece of architecture designed by Christian Michaelsen and Sigurd Rognstad. The exterior is a combination of brick and tile with sweeping pagoda-like towers. The building stands next to the Chinatown gate.

After the bust, the building stood vacant for half a decade. Some years before CASL planned to construct a new centralized building on Tan Court, Bernie had an idea that CASL could purchase the On Leong Building from the federal government. She pictured all of the space the corner building would allow CASL to improve and expand its programs. Bernie went to Esther and C. W. and proposed they buy the building to consolidate all of their separate properties under one roof.

C. W. and Esther felt it was a bad idea. Yes, there would be more space. Yes, it would be more centrally located now that the old railroad yards were being redeveloped north of Cermak. But C. W. and Esther knew CASL's clientele would feel wary about a building that came with so much baggage and perhaps bad luck. They believed it would be best to stay where they were on 24th Place and expand gradually as they saw fit. It was also the belief in Chinatown among residents and storeowners that only a religious group was in a position to purchase the building and turn around the gloom that fell over it after the FBI bust.

In 1993, the Chinese Christian Union Church put in a bid, along with a Buddhist organization, to buy the building. The Chinese Christian Union Church won and established the nonprofit Pui Tak Center. As Wu explained, "Pui Tak is a church community center that has an after-school program, a preschool, Chinese-language classes, and ESL classes, among others." Like CASL, it is also an Immigrant Welcoming Center.

David Wu was hired in 1994 as the executive director of the Pui Tak Center and has been in that position ever since. After Bernie retired, Wu became the longest tenured executive director of a social services agency in Chinatown. One of the first ways he set himself apart from CASL was by becoming instrumental in addressing the problems brought about by the new Indiana casinos in the early 1990s.

| | |

Casinos prey on people without a disposable income because, like the lottery, they can give people hope to earn riches with the scratch of a ticket or the pull of a slot machine. The Indiana casinos were built just over the Illinois border and targeted Chinatown residents because of the stereotype that Asians like to gamble.[2] While this label is used to "other" Asians and Asian Americans, the casinos preyed on low-income residents in Chinatown who felt isolated in Chicago and often lived alone by sending free buses to pick up people along the streets without designated stops or schedules. The casinos also enticed Chinatown residents with free chips and food.

The Chinatown Chamber of Commerce started noticing that local business was down. After quickly assessing the amount of people leaving Chinatown during the day and evenings—an area with twelve thousand residents at that time—the chamber realized that up to one thousand people would head to the casinos on any given day. This was a problem for Chinatown commerce, but it was also a safety issue. "It became dangerous for pedestrians," Wu said, speaking of the buses racing through narrow residential streets.

The casinos opened just before Pui Tak was founded, so this was an issue Wu walked into as he started his job as executive director. "I worked with other community groups to limit the casino buses to certain areas," Wu said. Pui Tak also runs a gambling awareness program to help educate both children and adults about the issues that can arise from gambling addiction. With dedicated social workers like David Wu, Chinatown has benefited from a continuity of leadership that understands both its changing needs as seen during the pandemic as well as those that remain consistent, like language classes, childcare, and counseling. "CASL is a large service leader, and at first I wanted to establish myself as the leader of Pui Tak and find my own niche," Wu said, "but I am proud to have come from CASL now."

Like David Wu, Grace Chan McKibben was hired for a summer job at CASL, teaching in the youth program in 1991. She went on to senior management positions at the University of Chicago, the Illinois Department of Employment

Security, and LaSalle Bank before returning to CASL in 2009 to become director of administration, a position she would hold for half a decade.

While at CASL during her second stint, Chan McKibben developed a close relationship with the Coalition for a Better Chinese American Community (CBCAC) because she had the most government and policy experience in her department.

After C. W. Chan founded CBCAC in 1998, the organization received its first grant and needed a financial sponsor to oversee these funds. CASL went on to fiscally sponsor CBCAC from 2000 to 2017 before it received 501(c)(3) status. Chan McKibben was hired in 2019 as CBCAC's first executive director. Before that, C. W. served CBCAC in the unpaid role of founder and chair.

| | |

Chicago has a tradition of honoring its most influential residents by naming a street after them. In 2016, Bernie's contributions to Chicago were recognized with the Honorary Bernarda "Bernie" Wong Way.

The unveiling of her honorary street included not only local politicians and CASL board members but also the people most connected to CASL on a daily basis: the seniors in the Adult Day Service and children in the preschool. Esther

From left to right: Esther Wong, Bernie Wong, and C. W. Chan, the three founders who stayed with CASL the longest. Without them, CASL and Chinatown would not be what they are today. Photo courtesy of the Chinese American Service League.

and C. W. joined Bernie in one of the many photo opportunities and it didn't escape them that they had all come such a long way since incorporating CASL as a nonprofit organization in 1978.

That same year, Bernie and Esther announced their respective retirements, and it was almost impossible to think of anyone who could replace their commitment and passion for the Chinatown community. By the time of her retirement, Bernie had also served as the first Asian American board member of United Way and the Chicago Public Library. She was recognized with awards from the Rainbow/PUSH Coalition, Mayor Richard M. Daley's Distinguished Community Leader, and President Barack Obama's "Winning the Future" initiative, just to name a few. Two of her office walls were covered with award certificates and plaques to honor her work over the decades.

James Mark Jr. was president of the CASL board when Bernie and Esther announced their retirements and understood that CASL was about to undergo its largest transformation yet. Mark is the nephew of longtime CASL board member Leonard Louie, and along with other board members like Ernie Wong and Brian Lee, he has a background in architecture and has devoted his career to creating public spaces. He worked on the field house at Ping Tom Park, which went on to be named for his uncle.

Traditionally, it's been very difficult to find someone to take over a leadership position after the founder of an organization has been the only person in that role for many decades. At CASL, that was even more pronounced because Esther had also been at CASL from the beginning, so Bernie's successor would not just be filling Bernie's shoes but Esther's, too. "I asked Esther to stay on one more year," Mark said, to help with the transition as the board set out to hire a new CEO. Esther reluctantly agreed.

But it wasn't just about finding a replacement for Bernie and Esther. There was another great worry. "History shows that succession leaders don't stay," Mark said. They usually find it impossible to follow in such illustrious footsteps and leave after a few years.

Mark and the CASL board spent a year planning for the search for Bernie's replacement and then another year to conduct the search, which reached out not just to both U.S. coasts but also to Canada. It proved difficult. "People didn't want to follow in Bernie's shoes," Mark recalled.

They ended up not needing to look very far from home. Paul Luu—who had been at the helm of the Vietnamese Association of Illinois in Uptown and before that had worked in many senior roles at the Boys & Girls Clubs throughout Chicago and in other parts of Illinois—was hired in 2017 as the new CEO of CASL.

"Paul really embraced Bernie," Mark said, "and continued in the same tradition to identify a need and make it happen."

Even so, the transition was not easy, most of all for Bernie. As Mark recalled, "It really broke my heart in the final few months. She was not ready to leave and teared up, not knowing how to give more at that point. But she did have so much more to give. Bernie and Esther were always thinking about the next steps."

Paul's determination to continue the agency's tradition of finding needs and creating programs became especially pronounced a couple of years after he became CEO of CASL.

PART V

New Challenges in the 2020s

19

Pandemic Response

In October 2019, Paul noticed a troubling development in China. An unknown virus had been discovered and no one was sure where it had originated. The symptoms were respiratory, causing people to have problems breathing, but those who fell ill also experienced fever, chills, and muscle aches.

As Paul read this news, he thought back to 2003 when SARS broke out in Hong Kong and quickly spread around the world. The 2003 SARS story caused him to pause and worry that this new virus could become a big problem and one that could easily reach the United States, including Chicago. There were a number of lessons learned from the 2003 SARS outbreak. One was that it was important to isolate suspected patients and make sure they didn't come into contact with others. The other was to contact trace and to find as many people who came into contact with the infected patients before the virus gets out of control. And the third was to wear face masks to prevent further spreading. SARS was frightening to those who contracted it and those who lived in areas with high transmission rates. It hit Hong Kong and southern China the most, places were CASL clients and staff often traveled to visit family and friends.

But for the most part, the world didn't come to a halt in 2003 and health-care officials around the globe flew to Hong Kong to help contain and to study it. People in Hong Kong, however, realized they never wanted to go through this again and started the practice of wearing face masks when they felt under the weather. It would be normal to see one or two people wearing face masks in an office setting or doctor's office.

Between 2003 and 2016, the U.S. government and many others around the world knew it wasn't a matter of if there would be another pandemic but when.

The Obama administration had put into place a clear pandemic response plan and was ready to spring into action if it happened during President Obama's two terms. It wasn't unusual for other organizations and groups to think about their own pandemic plans, especially if they remembered SARS in 2003.

Paul also realized something drastically different this time: the expansion and abundance of flight routes to and from China, Hong Kong, and the United States. Business and leisure travel across the Pacific had increased exponentially since 2003, especially when it came to Chicago. Chicago-based or -bound travelers had multiple choices for daily nonstop flights. In other words, air travel had reached a different level and the possibilities for sudden worldwide transmission seemed endless. It would be much more difficult to contact trace like the Hong Kong health officials had done in 2003. "Since a lot of our staff and clients travel back and forth between the U.S. and China, I started to wonder what would happen if it got to the U.S.," Paul recalled.

The winter holidays were approaching and those months were popular times for CASL staff and clients to return to Hong Kong and southern China because of their mild climates. "By November, my team and I had developed a four-stage shutdown plan in case we needed to use it," Paul recalled. "The different stages included planning according to developments within the U.S., Illinois, Cook County, and Chicago." If they never had to use this plan, so be it. At least they would have it for the future if what the epidemiologists had predicted eventually did come true.

Paul's executive team was happy with the plan they mapped out, and later in November, they presented it to the CASL board. The board voted to adopt it the following month. "My team and the board monitored developments in January and February, following the plan to a tee," Paul said. The news was not looking good.

Paul and his team knew they would need to be ready to go as fully remote as possible if there was indeed a complete shutdown of in-person services. Nothing like this had ever been done at CASL before, or in most of the United States for that matter. It wasn't like a snow day in Chicago, where conditions were so dangerous that it was too risky for staff and clients to come into the office for just a day or two. A shutdown would mean CASL staff would need to be able to continue their services remotely and as soon as feasibly possible after the shutdown started. To prepare for the worst-case scenario, CASL purchased hundreds of laptops for staff if they needed to work remotely. CASL also improved its broadband capabilities and trained staff in using online platforms like Zoom to connect with clients at home.

"In January and February 2020, CASL invested in tens of thousands of masks and sanitizer in five-gallon barrels placed in storage, as well as tens of thousands of plastic gloves and aprons for staff to wear on home visits to seniors if there was the need," Paul said. It was an investment well spent, they felt. With the senior apartments just across the street from CASL, it would be easy and convenient for staff to pick up this personal protective equipment (PPE) to visit clients. The CASL executive team put into place a staff training program to teach them what to do in case of a shutdown. "People complained about it," Paul said. Some viewed it as alarmist and even a waste of staff time.

But then on Sunday, March 15, 2022, Illinois governor J. B. Pritzker, along with governors around the country, called on their residents to start teaching, learning, and working remotely unless they were essential workers. "CASL was ready to go fully remote on Monday, March 16, 2020," Paul said. "We were at 100 percent capacity while other nonprofits were not prepared and struggled starting March 16th."

| | |

By the middle of June 2020, some CASL clients were having a difficult time coping with these new circumstances. Many lived alone and felt more isolated when they were told not to go out at all unless to buy groceries or other essentials. CASL wanted to accommodate them and provide the assistance these clients needed, so in mid-June 2020, the agency was able to open with 20 percent of their staff back in person. "CASL was one of the very few social service agencies that could do this because others suffered employee illness and even death," Paul recalled. It wasn't difficult for CASL's staff and clients to wear masks since this practice had been normal in Hong Kong and China for almost two decades. Although CASL staff and clients were Chicago residents, many had the opportunity to visit family and friends in Hong Kong and China over the years and would have seen others wearing masks on these visits.

CASL was also on top of things with the rollout of the first doses of the COVID-19 vaccine. "In February 2021, CASL worked to get all of the staff vaccinated because many lived in three-generation households," Paul said. "Vaccines were brought on-site for the first dose and CASL connected with the Chicago Health Department and area clinics to get people their second dose." With the whole staff vaccinated, CASL felt better about providing services to clients.

But CASL didn't just look out for its staff and clients. It also helped area social service agencies, especially in January 2021 when Paul heard from his counterparts in other organizations that they didn't have enough masks for their staff and clients and were struggling to find ways to meet this growing need. At the beginning of the pandemic, people were told to wear cloth masks because the surgical and N95 masks were needed for health-care workers and other essential workers. But by early 2021, it was getting more apparent that cloth masks were not as helpful in preventing the spread of the virus as were medical-grade masks. "A CASL board member secured a purchase of 250,000 masks when PPP loans were not yet available," Paul said. "These agencies were struggling to keep staff safe, so CASL donated 35,000 to 40,000 masks to Chinatown businesses and other AAPI [Asian American and Pacific Islander] organizations." This timing coincided with the height of the anti-Asian crime wave during the early part of the pandemic. CASL also donated more masks to forty to fifty social service agencies, each time giving out five thousand, ten thousand, or twenty thousand masks, depending on their needs. "Eighty percent went to the south and west sides, serving Black and Latinx communities," Paul said.

And then there was food. The pandemic caused great shortages in food supplies and many residents in Chinatown did not have enough to eat. CASL's elderly clients and their adult children also expressed this worry. It was difficult to purchase food, especially healthy food. "In April 2020, Chinatown community leaders called me because the meal programs in Chinatown were losing money and there wasn't enough food to go around," Paul said. "Food insecurity was a huge problem and people were afraid to go outside because of the virus and the backlash against Asians."

Since CASL already had industrial kitchens capable of preparing food for hundreds of clients at a time, Paul and his executive team spent a week in the spring of 2020 converting the second-floor chef-training kitchen into a senior meals kitchen. "The culinary students started to make three hot, culturally appropriate meals each day for 350 seniors in six buildings in the area," Paul recalled. To accomplish all of this, CASL received funding to allow its recent culinary program graduates to work in the CASL kitchen for twelve to fourteen hours a week. With licenses in hand, these recent grads met with job counselors when they weren't in the CASL kitchen and worked on finding permanent jobs that paid better.

By the summer of 2022, CASL received $1 million through Senator Dick Durbin's office to provide senior meals not just in Chinatown but also in Black and Latinx communities around Chicago. "So instead of reaching 350 seniors a day, the program will be able to help six hundred to seven hundred seniors a day," Paul said. CASL also secured $5 million from the state of Illinois to build another industrial kitchen and childcare center at a to-be-determined space.

20

The End of an Era

In early 2019 when this book project started, Bernie and Esther had been retired for a couple of years. Bernie and Albert had just returned from a two-month trip to celebrate their fiftieth wedding anniversary, traveling to Hong Kong, Singapore, Australia, and New Zealand. Upon their return, Bernie noted that she was having trouble breathing. It turned out her right lung was three-fourths filled with liquid and she needed to have it drained before it collapsed. Even worse, she also learned her breast cancer from the late 1980s had returned.

But nothing could have prepared Bernie for the phone call she received at home while recuperating from surgery. Her husband, Albert, had suffered a fatal heart attack while playing Ping-Pong, one of the activities that brought together the ten original CASL founders. Albert had stood by Bernie from the very beginning of CASL, even when it was just a fantastic idea at the friends' potluck dinners. He was always a willing participant at different CASL activities, so much so that staff and clients had become part of the Wong family over all these decades. People often joked that their daughter, Jacinta, had another sibling and that sibling was CASL.

Newly widowed and mourning Albert's death, Bernie couldn't keep away from CASL even though she was battling cancer. She continued to visit the different departments and attend events put on by the seniors. She also joined the Pine Tree Senior Council. But by 2020, her cancer had spread and she felt the added stress of the pandemic. Soon, Bernie was no longer allowed to leave the house due to her failing health. Yet the CASL executive team was never far from Bernie's heart or ear, and she was kept up to date on their COVID-19 mitigations and all of the efforts CASL took to vaccinate staff, provide meals to seniors, and continue services remotely.

By 2021, it was clear that Bernie's cancer was rapidly spreading and getting progressively worse. She tried treatment after treatment, all to no avail. Bernie's strength and energy remained high given her diagnosis, but it became apparent in early spring 2021 that the end was near. On April 27, 2021, Bernie passed away at home surrounded by Jacinta, her brother Albert, and his wife, Selina. Two days later, former president Barack Obama tweeted about her death. "Bernie Wong was a trailblazer who spent her life advocating for Asian Americans and immigrant communities in Chicago and across the U.S. Her legacy of community leadership inspired me and so many others, and her impact will be felt for generations to come."[1]

Despite strict COVID-19 restrictions that made funeral arrangements difficult, her funeral and memorial service at St. Therese Church in Chinatown pushed the limits of COVID-19 capacity and attracted notables like long-term friends Illinois senator Dick Durbin, Cook County Board of Commissioners president Toni Preckwinkle, Congressman Danny Davis, Illinois State Representative Theresa Mah, and of course, Linda Yu and Esther Wong, all of whom spoke so fondly about Bernie, the "Dynamo from Hong Kong." This outpouring of love was a testament to Bernie's commitment to CASL, Chinatown, Chicago, Illinois, and the United States.

The autumn of 2022 saw another great loss for CASL. Esther passed away, also from cancer. Esther had devoted most of her adult life to CASL, always following her motto of honoring her profession and cherishing her relationships. Esther was also a proud member of CASL's Pine Tree Senior Council. So it's in her and Bernie's memory that all author proceeds of this book will be donated to the Pine Tree Senior Council.

Even though Bernie and Esther are no longer here to check on their fruits of almost half a century of dedication to the Chinese communities in Chicago, their legacy and that of the other founders is evident in many ways. Whereas they started in 1978 not knowing how to reach people in the Chinatown community to provide much-needed services, now forty-five years later CASL has become the largest employer in Chinatown and the go-to place for new immigrants and families who need childcare, senior care, or one of the many other services the agency provides. At the time of writing, CASL employed over six hundred staff, most of whom are bilingual, and served thousands of families of all ages and backgrounds each year.

Epilogue
Looking Forward

Chicago's Chinatown has become a destination for locals and visitors from out of town. It's also home to many new immigrants who are able to purchase their own houses or condos thanks to efforts against displacement from gentrification and CASL's housing programs. Although CASL isn't solely responsible for the growth of Chinatown, it's difficult to imagine what Chinatown and its surrounding area would have looked like without CASL's influence. The Chinatown Library, Chinese American Museum of Chicago, Ping Tom Park, and the Zhou B. Art Center in neighboring Bridgeport have all been touched by CASL.

CASL is changing, too. The agency recently rewrote its mission statement to look beyond Chinatown. It has initiated the Change InSight data clearinghouse to work with AAPI and other immigrant communities around the country. AAPI communities are the fastest growing demographic in the United States, but because they are all lumped together when it comes to federal government statistics, there is no way to assess specific needs among these different communities. Without accurate data, AAPI communities are at risk of losing out on federal, state, and local funding. Change InSight will help to fix this problem.

Illinois also saw a great advancement in 2021 when it passed the Teaching Equitable Asian American Community History (TEAACH) Act, the first of its kind in the United States. Not only was CASL a strong supporter of the TEAACH legislation before it was signed into law, but it also had connections to Asian Americans Advancing Justice/Chicago, which has helped develop curricula to be used in Illinois public schools to meet the TEAACH standards. Asian Americans Advancing Justice began in 1992 as the Asian American Institute, with which Bernie and Esther were both involved. Theresa Mah, the first Asian American Illinois

state representative, has been a great friend to CASL and was a cosponsor of the
TEAACH Act and helped obtain funding to build a Chinatown high school, the
plans for which are still uncertain at the time of writing.

And although still grossly underreported, instances of anti-Asian hate crimes
have increased exponentially from the start of the COVID-19 pandemic. In 2021,
the Asian American Foundation chose CASL to operate an Anti-Hate Action
Center to compile data, work with law enforcement and elected officials, provide
mental health and legal services to victims, as well as other means of support to
victims and their families.

As much as CASL is looking to the future, the pandemic is not over and at
the time of writing, it's difficult to tell when that will happen. With all the stress
over contracting the virus, fear of anti-Asian hate, food insecurity, and job loss or
extended periods of unpaid days out of work, the mental health of Chinatown
residents has taken a huge toll.

To meet this growing need, CASL has started a new behavioral health center.
CASL understands that this subject is still taboo in the Chinese community, yet
knows there's never been a greater need for these services, which are available to
people of all ages, not just seniors.

In the summer of 2023, CASL announced a generous grant from David Cotton and the Sue Ling Gin Foundation to build a new comprehensive facility in
the neighboring Bridgeport–McKinley Park area. As it's proven over the decades,
when CASL sees a need, it finds a way to serve.

This philosophy is exactly what Bernie, Esther, C. W., and the other seven CASL
founders had in mind when they delivered their first program over four decades
ago. Which leads to another question: Did the founders come together by fate, or
yuan fen as it's called in Mandarin? Would CASL be here today if Eleanor So hadn't
first volunteered in Chinatown or if Bernie hadn't quit her secure job and taken a
chance on a start-up? Would CASL have made a name for itself in a way that its
services would be desired outside the boundaries of Chinatown if it weren't for
Esther Wong's and C. W. Chan's long dedication to the agency and community?
And would new immigrants these days even devote their lives to helping others
when there are so many well-paying jobs available in today's high-tech world?

Perhaps these questions will be answered over CASL's next half century.

Acknowledgments

Linda Yu was my first interview subject, which, looking back, seems like a naive choice when most of the other people I spoke with were not Emmy award–winning broadcast journalists. So, thank you, Linda, for all the time you spent talking to me and for agreeing to write the lovely foreword of this book. It has been a pure joy working with you!

Massive thanks to Bernie Wong and Esther Wong. May their memories be a blessing. When it came to interviewing other CASL cofounders, I am grateful that I already knew Heidi and C. W. Chan from our Chinese University of Hong Kong Alumni Association. C. W., thank you for talking to me about your early years in Chinatown and for your dedication to the community and to Chicago as a whole. We are all better off because of you.

Jacinta, thank you a million for all your lovely memories, photos, and help with this book. Getting to know you has been one of the greatest joys during this project.

Thanks also to Grace Chiu, Iris Ho, Anna Ho, and Eleanor So for speaking to me about your time in Chicago and how each of you made indelible contributions to CASL that can still be seen today, long after you moved away from Chicago. A huge thank-you to Paul Ho for his memories of CASL that he relayed to me through Anna.

Paul Luu, I cannot thank you enough for all your help with this book and for speaking with me specifically about all that CASL has tackled during the pandemic and the rise of anti-Asian hate. Your work is invaluable. Thank you also to Brandi Adams and Elizabeth Bishop for providing me with access to CASL's archives.

You made my job much easier than it would have been without these precious resources.

Valerie Jarrett, thank you for your correspondence during the early stages of this book and for your support to CASL throughout the decades. Tina Tchen, my heartfelt gratitude for your memories of working with CASL and Bernie. Monica Tang, thank you for your recollections of your long tenure at CASL and for putting me in touch with so many people instrumental to CASL's success, including Ruby Chan, Catalina Chan, Hoi Wai Chua, and Ken Tsang and family. Your fact-checking is invaluable!

Brian Lee, thank you for telling me about your early years in Chicago and how Bernie brought you on to the CASL board. Gordon Chin, thank you for speaking with me from San Francisco about your work there and your collaborations with Bernie and CASL. I am also deeply grateful for your advice about publishing a book about community social service agencies and was proud to use your book as a source.

Herman So, thank you for answering my query from out of the blue to talk about your family's early years in the United States and your relationship with CASL. And thank you for answering my many LinkedIn messages whenever new questions popped into my mind. I am so honored to tell your story and will be forever grateful for your assistance. I could not think of a more heartfelt story to begin this book.

Larry So, thank you for speaking to me from Macau. I so enjoyed learning from you about your work with CASL and your dedication to seniors in Chicago. Dr. K. K. Wan, thank you for your lessons on Chinatown history, your recollections of the early months of CASL, and for your generosity in providing CASL with its first Chinatown office space so many decades ago.

Mary McKay, thank you for telling me about Bernie's work as an alumnae with the Brown School at Washington University. Your account gave me a greater picture of Bernie's dedication to students from afar. Paul Cusimano, thank you for giving me a great picture of the office atmosphere at CASL, especially during the large fundraising drives. This information was invaluable and I am grateful to you for your time.

Much gratitude to the Zhou Brothers, ShanZuo and DaHuang, for your lovely words about Bernie and CASL. Thank you to Clare Huang for translating the Zhou Brothers' statement. Rosaline Lee, thank you so much for your touching memories about your friendship with Bernie and your college years together. Ray Spaeth passed away as I was putting the finishing touches on this book and I will always remember the hours he spent speaking with me about his years with CASL and about Chinatown in the 1970s. Jerry Erickson, thank you for your statement about your work with CASL and Bernie. Elaine Sit, it was such a pleasure to talk to you about your father's life and his work in Chinatown. Darryl Tom, thank you for your e-mails.

Kam Liu, thank you so much for talking to me about your support of CASL and your family's generous donation. I immensely enjoyed learning about your early years in Chinatown. Albert Lo, thank you so much for talking on the phone with me and for being such a great resource about your family's history. Thank you also for fielding my WhatsApp messages when I had questions.

Paul Igasaki, thank you for sharing your stories about Bernie and Chicago. I truly appreciate the time you took to speak with me. Yman Vien, thank you for speaking to me about the Chinese Mutual Aid Association and refugee resettlement. Dim sum awaits!

At Studio Gang, my sincere gratitude to Josh Ellman, Alissa Anderson, and Andi Altenbach for providing me with materials about Jeanne Gang's work with CASL.

Much gratitude to Ben Lau and David Wu for sharing your experiences at CASL and how it inspired both of you to make a difference in other realms in Chinatown. I appreciate the time you both took to speak with me. Brenda Arksey, thank you for providing me with almost all of the information about the different early childhood education services. Ricky Lam, thank you so much for speaking with me about your long career at CASL and the inner workings of your department.

Former CASL presidents Ernie Wong and Jim Mark, thank you for your wonderful recollections of Bernie and of your work on the CASL board. David Wong, thank you for telling me about your parents' dedication to CASL. The agency would not be the same without the care and attention of Art and Elaine Wong.

More thanks to Joan and Raymond So, Xixuan Collins for your friendship and the book's title, and Gloria Chao. Jean Iversen, I'm so honored you were willing to beta read these chapters and have loved going through this process with you. The sidebars are here because of you!

Martha Bayne, it has been a tremendous honor and delight to work with you on this book. I could not wish for a more enthusiastic editor. A huge thank-you to Dominique Moore for passing on my proposal to Martha. And thank you to Mariah Mendes Schaefer, Kevin Cunningham, Joyce Li, and Megan Donnan for all your attentive assistance. Thank you Jennie Fisher for the beautiful cover! Bill Nelson, thank you for creating a gorgeous map of Chicago's Chinatown and the many places CASL has called home.

And finally to my family, Tom, Jake, Rachel, and Martin, all of whom have become part of the CASL family in one way or another. Words cannot express how much I appreciate your love and support.

I made every effort to tell this story as accurately as possible, but any errors in this book are mine and mine alone.

All author proceeds will be donated to the Pine Tree Senior Council at the Chinese American Service League.

Appendix I

Chinese American Service League Board of Directors, 1978–2022

Tenny Ahn
Greg Barr
Hong Brunner
Ram B. Cabanero
Peter Carey
Chun Wah "C. W." Chan, board president from 1978 to 1986
Daisy Chan
Heidi Chan
Mark Chan, board president from 1987 to 1993
Sai Kit Chan
Winnie Chan
Nancy Chen
Eileen Chin
Vivian L. Chin
Christopher Chiu
Grace Chiu
Gay-Young Cho
Victoria Chou
Christine Chun
Chi Cuong Chung
Linval Chung
Martin Connolly
Judy Curry
John Czyzycki
Margaret Dolan

Xinqi Dong
Karen Eng
A. Gerald Erickson
Anne Fan
Normal Finkel
Bonnie Fong, board president from 2022 to present
Rita Fong
Roger Fong
Cheong Fung
Edward D. Gin
Jennie Gin
Sue Ling Gin
Stephen E. Gohres
Lily Moy Gulik
Dawn Haghighi
Kevin Hall
Anna Ho
Iris Ho
Paul Ho
Jerry Hong
Wellington Hsu
Canfield K. Ip
Michelle Jacobson
Chaoran Jin
Lucinda Lee Katz
Miroslava Mejia Krug

Eric Kwok
Joseph H. Kye
Denise Lam
Jed Lam
Vernon Lam
Yvonne Lau
Allen C. L. Lee
Brian Lee
David Lee
Gene Lee
Winkle Lee
Raymond B. Lee
Gary J. Leong
Angelina Li
Maria C. Lin
Kam L. Liu
Leonard Louie
Sister Sheila Lyne
Michael S. Marcus
James Mark Jr., board president from
    2015 to 2021
Ron Mark
Robert K. Masuda
Jieu Mauk
Charles T. Menghini
Alfred Moy
Jeffrey Moy
Helen Moy
Mabel Lee Moy
Constance Murphy
Karen Ng
Paul Ngai
Paul Pai
Sarah Pang
Julia Tang Peters
Allen Rafalson
Mike Rettaliata
Allen Rodriguez
Larry Rosenzweig

Vern Sandacz
Frank Scumacci
Victor Shane
Ramsay Shu
Grace Sielaff
Eleanor So
Raymond Spaeth II
Tina Tchen
Darryl Tom
Larry Toy
Kim H. Tran
Marilyn Fatt Vitale
Erikka Wang
Sona Wang
Kathy Wing
Arthur Wong, board president from
    1998 to 2008
Bernarda "Bernie" Wong, board presi-
    dent 1978
David Wong
Ernest Wong, board president from
    2009 to 2015
Esther Wong
Fuk Chun Alan Wong
Gertrude M. Wong
James M. Wong
Jok Wong
Philip Wong, board president from 1994
    to 1997
Quincy Wong
Stanley Wong
Cora Yang
Virginia I. Yang
Sevila Yee
Ann Yeung
Francis Yip
Henry Yon
Betsy W. Young

Appendix II

List of Interviews and Written Statements

Phone or Zoom Interviews

Brenda Arksey, June 2022
C. W. Chan, May 6, 2021, July 13, 2022
Mike Chan, August 19, 2021
Gordon Chin, May 7, 2021
Grace Chiu, May 14, 2021
Paul Cusimano, May 10, 2021
Anna Ho, May 5, 2021
Iris Ho, May 19, 2021
Stacy Huang, May 14, 2021
Paul Igasaki, May 27, 2022
Ricky Lam, August 31, 2022
Ben Lau, July 23, 2022
Brian Lee, May 7, 2021
Kam L. Liu, June 16, 2021
Albert Lo, September 8, 2021
Paul Luu, July 16, 2019, June 13, 2022

Mary McKay, May 7, 2021
James Mark, September 16, 2022
Elaine Sit, May 3, 2022
Eleanor So, May 21, 2021
Herman So, June 17, 2021
Larry So, June 15, 2021
Raymond Spaeth, June 12, 2021
Tina Tchen, May 24, 2021
Yman Vien, August 2, 2022
Dr. K. K. Wan, June 4, 2021
Bernie Wong, July 16, 2019
Ernest Wong, September 4, 2022
Esther Wong, July 16, 2019
Jacinta Wong, June 18, 2021
David Wu, July 26, 2022
Linda Yu, May 5, 2021

Written Statements and Emails

Catalina Chan, June 6, 2021
Hoi Wai Chua, May 31, 2021
Jerry Erickson, June 8, 2021, June 15, 2021
Rosaline Lee, June 19, 2021
Albert Lo, September 12, 2021, September 13, 2021, September 30, 2022
Grace Chan McKibben, September 15, 2022

Mitchell M. Obstfield on behalf of the Zhou Brothers, May 12, 2021
Herman So, May 7, 2022, June 9 2022
Monica Tang, May 16, 2021, May 20, 2021, August 1, 2022, August 31, 2022, September 2, 2022, September 5, 2022
Ken Tsang and family, June 5, 2021
Esther Wong, September 3, 2022

Notes

Chapter 1. Hong Kong Connections

1. Timothy Gilfoyle, "Serving Chicago: Interviews with Mary Dempsey and Bernie Wong," *Chicago History* 39, no. 3 (2014): 70.
2. "Interview with Bernarda Wong," Chinese Women of America 1848–1982 Research Project, June 6, 1982, 4.
3. "Interview with Bernarda Wong," 5.
4. "Interview with Bernarda Wong," 5.
5. "Interview with Bernarda Wong," 5.
6. "Interview with Bernarda Wong," 5.
7. "Chinese Women of America 1848–1982 Research Project," Chinese Culture Foundation of San Francisco, February 24, 1983, 2.
8. "Chinese Women of America 1848–1982 Research Project," 5.
9. "Chinese Women of America 1848–1982 Research Project," 6.
10. "Chinese Women of America 1848–1982 Research Project," 6.
11. "Chinese Women of America 1848–1982 Research Project," 7.
12. "Chinese Women of America 1848–1982 Research Project," 7.
13. Statement from Rosaline Lee Fung, June 2021.
14. "Chinese Women of America 1848–1982 Research Project," 10.

Chapter 4. The Dentist's Office

1. Simpson, *Rogues, Rebels, and Rubber Stamps*, 164.
2. Paul M. Green and Melvin G. Holli, *The Mayors: The Chicago Political Tradition*, 4th ed. (Carbondale: University of Southern Illinois Press), 165.

Chapter 5. A Tale of Two Chinatowns

1. Jean Iversen, *Local Flavor: Restaurants That Shaped Chicago's Neighborhoods* (Evanston, IL: Northwestern University Press, 2018), 5.

2. Chuimei Ho and Soo Lon Moy, eds., *Chinese in Chicago: 1870–1945* (San Francisco: Arcadia Publishing, 2005), 63.

3. Emma Graves Fitzsimmons, "Wayne C. Sit: 1918–2006," *Chicago Tribune*, October 30, 2006.

Chapter 6. In the Spirit of the Settlement Movement

1. Peggy Glowacki and Julia Hendry, *Hull-House: Images of America* (San Francisco: Arcadia Publishing, 2004), 7.

2. Jane Addams, *Twenty Years at Hull-House with Autobiographical Notes* (Cutchogue, NY: Buccaneer Books, 1994), 56.

3. Gordon Chin, *Building Community, Chinatown Style: A Half Century of Leadership in San Francisco Chinatown* (San Francisco: Friends of Chinatown Community Development Center, 2015).

4. Lev Golinkin, *A Backpack, a Bear, and Eight Crates of Vodka: A Memoir* (New York: Doubleday, 2014), 223.

5. Graydon Megan, "Edwin Silverman, Led State Office for Refugees and Immigrants, Dies," *Chicago Tribune*, September 21, 2017.

Chapter 7. Linda Yu to the Rescue

1. "5 Workers Killed in Chicago Plunge," *New York Times*, December 12, 1981, 10.

2. Chinese American Service League, *Annual Report* (Chicago: Chinese American Service League, 1985), 3.

3. Dorothy Samachson, "Agency Profile: Chinese American Service League Answers Needs in Chinatown," *The Trust Quarterly*, Summer 1992, 25.

Chapter 10. The Next Generation of Social Workers

1. Written statement from Yung Chan, May 2021.

2. Casey Banas and Devonda Byers, "Education Chief: City Schools Worst," *Chicago Tribune*, November 8, 1987.

3. Banas and Byers, "Education Chief."

4. Written statement from Catalina Chan, July 6, 2021.

Chapter 11. The Zhou Brothers Plant Roots in Chicago

1. From a statement from the Zhou brothers in May 2021, translated from the Chinese by Clare Huang.

Chapter 13. Expanding Senior Services

1. Ted Shen, "Cheung, Lam Give Boost to Chinese-American League," *Chicago Tribune*, October 9, 1994.

Chapter 15. CASL Needs a New Home

1. Blair Kamin, "Chinatown Center a Rich Design for Immigrants," *Chicago Tribune*, July 4, 2004, Arts & Entertainment section, 12.

2. Cheryl Kent, "Screen Play: A Community Center by Studio Gang Architects Connects Chicago to Its Chinese heritage," *Architecture*, December 2004, 90.

3. Jeanne Gang, "Studio Gang, Chicago, USA," *A+T New Materiality II* (2004): 122.

4. Kamin, "Chinatown Center," 1.

5. Gang, "Studio Gang, Chicago," 122.

6. Kamin, "Chinatown Center," 12.

7. John E. Czarnecki, "Taking a Leap of Faith," *Architectural Record*, December 2002, 76.

8. Czarnecki, "Taking a Leap of Faith," 76.

Chapter 17. Multigenerational Services in One Space

1. Ian Volner, "Chicago Public Library, Chinatown Branch," *Architect: The Journal of the American Institute of Architects*, April 12, 2016.

Chapter 18. CASL's Impact and Recognition

1. Pui Tak Center, "About," https://www.puitak.org/en/history.

2. Mia Han Colby et al., "Unpacking the Root Causes of Gambling in the Asian Community: Contesting the Myth of the Asian Gambling Culture," *Frontiers in Public Health*, November 3, 2022.

Chapter 20. The End of an Era

1. https://twitter.com/BarackObama/status/1387908687830949894.

Bibliography

"5 Workers Killed in Chicago Plunge." *New York Times*, December 12, 1981, 10.

Addams, Jane. *Twenty Years at Hull-House with Autobiographical Notes*. Cutchogue, NY: Buccaneer Books, 1994.

Alznauer, Amy, ShanZuo Zhou, and DaHuang Zhou. *Flying Paintings: The Zhou Brothers: A Story of Revolution and Art*. Somerville, MA: Candlewick Press, 2020.

Banas, Casey, and Devonda Byers. "Education Chief: City Schools Worst." *Chicago Tribune*, November 8, 1987.

Bird, Les. *Along the Southern Boundary: A Marine Police Officer's Frontline Account of the Vietnamese Boatpeople and Their Arrival in Hong Kong*. Hong Kong: Blacksmith Books, 2021.

Burton, Thomas M., and David Silverman. "Chinatown Building Seized in Raid." *Chicago Tribune*, June 17, 1988.

Byrne, Jane. *My Chicago*, New York: Norton, 1992.

Chang, Iris. *The Chinese in America: A Narrative History*. New York: Penguin, 2003.

Chin, Gordon. *Building Community, Chinatown Style: A Half Century of Leadership in San Francisco Chinatown*. San Francisco: Friends of Chinatown Community Development Center, 2015.

Chinese American Service League. *Annual Report*. Chicago: Chinese American Service League, 1980, 1985, 1988, 1990–95, 1997–99, 2004, 2006, 2008–10, 2014–21. [CASL Archive]

"Chinese Women of America 1848–1982 Research Project." Chinese Culture Foundation of San Francisco, February 24, 1983.

Colby, Mia Han, Ben Hires, Lisette Le, Dawn Sauma, Man Yoyo Yau, MyDzung Thi Chu, and Heang Leung Rubin. "Unpacking the Root Causes of Gambling in the Asian Community: Contesting the Myth of the Asian Gambling Culture." *Frontiers in Public Health*, November 3, 2022.

Czarnecki, John E. "Taking a Leap of Faith." *Architectural Record*, December 2002, 73–78.

Dod, R. Bruce. "When Jane Byrne Was Elected Mayor." *Chicago Tribune*, November, 14, 2014.

Eng, Monica. "What a Murder in My Family Reveals about Chicago's Chinese Gangs." WBEZ Chicago, May 5, 2018.

Fitzsimmons, Emma Graves. "Wayne C. Sit: 1918–2006." *Chicago Tribune*, October 30, 2006.

Gang, Jeanne. *Reveal: Studio Gang Architects*. New York: Princeton Architectural Press, 2011.

Gang, Jeanne. "Studio Gang, Chicago, USA." *A+T New Materiality II* (2004): 112–29.

Gang, Jeanne, and Zoe Ryan, eds. *Building Inside/Studio Gang Architects*. Chicago: Studio Gang Architects, 2012.

Gilfoyle, Timothy. "Serving Chicago: Interviews with Mary Dempsey and Bernie Wong." *Chicago History* 39, no. 3 (2014): 68–80.

Glowacki, Peggy, and Julia Hendry. *Hull-House: Images of America*. San Francisco: Arcadia Publishing, 2004.

Golinkin, Lev. *A Backpack, a Bear, and Eight Crates of Vodka: A Memoir*. New York: Doubleday, 2014.

Green, Paul M., and Melvin G. Holli. *The Mayors: The Chicago Political Tradition*. 4th ed. Carbondale: Southern Illinois University Press, 2013.

Hautzinger, Daniel. "Architect Brian Lee Brings the Expertise Required for Skyscrapers to Neighborhood Buildings." WTTW, June 9, 2022. https://interactive.wttw.com/playlist/2022/06/09/brian-lee-architect

Ho, Chuimei, and Soo Lon Moy. *Chinese in Chicago, 1870–1945*. San Francisco: Arcadia Publishing, 2005.

Hsu, Hua. "The Many Lives of Vincent Chin." *New Yorker*, June 23, 2022.

Iversen, Jean. *Local Flavor: Restaurants That Shaped Chicago's Neighborhoods*. Evanston, IL: Northwestern University Press, 2018.

Kamin, Blair. "Chinatown Center a Rich Design for Immigrants." *Chicago Tribune*, July 4, 2004, Arts & Entertainment section, 1, 12–13.

Kent, Cheryl. "Screen Play: A Community Center by Studio Gang Architects Connects Chicago to Its Chinese Heritage." *Architecture*, December 2004, 90–95.

Kinkead, Gwen. *Chinatown*. New York: Harper Collins, 1992.

Ling, Huping. *Chinese Chicago: Race, Transnational Migration and Community since 1870*. Stanford: Stanford University Press, 2012.

Marriner, James. "A Tale of Two Felons." *Chicago Reader*, December 24, 1998.

Megan, Graydon. "Edwin Silverman, Led State Office for Refugees and Immigrants, Dies." *Chicago Tribune*, September 21, 2017.

Morens, David M., and Anthony S. Fauci. "Emerging Pandemic Diseases: How We Got to COVID-19." *Cell*, August 15, 2020.

Polacheck, Hilda Satt. *I Came a Stranger: The Story of a Hull-House Girl*. Urbana: University of Illinois Press, 1989.

Rosenthal, Elisabeth. "The SARS Epidemic: The Path; from China's Provinces, a Crafty Germ Breaks Out," *New York Times*, April 27, 2003.

Samachson, Dorothy. "Agency Profile: Chinese American Service League Answers Needs in Chinatown." *The Trust Quarterly*, Summer 1992.

Shen, Ted. "Cheung, Lam Give Boost to Chinese-American League." *Chicago Tribune*, October 9, 1994.

Simpson, Dick. *Rogues, Rebels, and Rubber Stamps: The Politics of the Chicago City Council from 1863 to the Present*. Boulder: Westview, 2001.

"Vietnamese Reviving a Chicago Slum." *New York Times*, January 2, 1986.

Volner, Ian. "Chicago Public Library, Chinatown Branch." *Architect: The Journal of the American Institute of Architects*, April 12, 2019.

Wang, Qian Julie. *Beautiful Country: A Memoir*. New York: Doubleday, 2021.

Yu, Ignatius T. S., Yuguo Li, Tze Wai Wong, Wilson Tam, Andy T. Chan, Joseph H. W. Lee, Dennis Y. C. Leung, and Tommy Ho. "Evidence of Airborne Transmission of the Severe Acute Respiratory Syndrome Virus." *New England Journal of Medicine* 350 (2004): 1731–39.

Index

Susan Blumberg-Kason is the author of *Bernardine's Shanghai Salon: The Story of the Doyenne of Old China* and *Good Chinese Wife: A Love Affair with China Gone Wrong.*

The University of Illinois Press
is a founding member of the
Association of University Presses.

Composed in 10.25/14 Adobe Garamond Pro
with Frutiger LT Std display
by Lisa Connery
at the University of Illinois Press
Manufactured by Versa Press, Inc.

University of Illinois Press
1325 South Oak Street
Champaign, IL 61820–6903
www.press.uillinois.edu